"The Bible says that 'what you sow, you shall reap,' but I believe that it goes much deeper than that."

Pieter Van Der Westhuizen

BREAKING THE ZONE

Pieter Van Der Westhuizen

Tribute Publishing
2017

Copyright © 2017
Tribute Publishing
Frisco, Texas U.S.A

Tribute
Publishing

Breaking the Zone
First Edition January 2017

All Worldwide Rights Reserved
ISBN: 978-0-9982860-2-0

All Rights Reserved. No part of this book may be reproduced, stored in a retrieval system, or transmitted, in any form, or by any means, electronic, mechanical, recorded, photocopied, or otherwise, without the prior written permission of the copyright owner, except by a reviewer who may quote brief passages in a review.

To Sarah
Thank you for believing in me.

Table of Contents

Preface i

Chapter 1 – Where It All Started 1

Chapter 2 – The Crash That Made Me Move 11

Chapter 3 – Finding Yourself 25

Chapter 4 – The Challenge of Networking 33

Chapter 5 – Procrastination: The Dream Killer 47

Chapter 6 – Believe in Yourself 57

Chapter 7 – Prepare Yourself 69

Chapter 8 – Creating Opportunities Through Networking 79

Chapter 9 – Teach 91

Chapter 10 – Never Stop Learning 109

Chapter 11 – Always Strive for More 119

Acknowledgements 133

About the Author 137

Preface

We have all felt lost at some stage in our lives. We feel lost with what we want out of life, what we want to do for the rest of our lives, or just wondering what the meaning of life is. We feel stuck in a rut and don't know how to get out of it, or we are too scared to change anything.

I must say, that was definitely the case for me!

I had a fairly uneventful childhood and grew up in a small coal mining village outside Witbank, South Africa. Nothing much ever happened there and children were still able to play outside anywhere in the village without any fear or trepidation. Being the youngest of five children with the closest sibling four years older than me, I spent most of my time alone using my creativity to have as much fun as possible.

We were not a wealthy family, as you can imagine with five children and my mother being a homemaker. The one thing we were never short on was love. I can truly say that I never had to wonder if my parents loved me. However, because of our financial position, my father, being a diesel mechanic, did private jobs, car repairs, and panel beating after working hours to earn an extra income. There was nothing my dad couldn't do. If it had wheels, he could fix it. Unfortunately, because of this, my parents were never present for sporting events or any periods of significance to me. I initially thought that that did not bother me, but as years went by and I saw how other parents were involved in their children's lives, I felt more alone and kind of worthless.

My parents sometimes borrowed money from some of my friend's parents and always told me to go pick up the money from them. This caused me to feel embarrassed and in turn made me feel even worse about myself. I started to creep deeper into my protective shell, especially when they were late paying back the money and my friend's parents would ask me when they would be getting back their money.

Another of my friends had a very strict father and for some reason or other, he liked to belittle me. Whenever his son wanted to come to my house to play or for a sleepover, he always told his son that I had to come and ask him personally. He would then let me stand in front of him and ask the question. Then, he would just stare at me with a disapproving look and say, "NO!" I never understood why he wanted me to ask him if he knew he was going to say 'no' in the first place. I hated that so much. Due to that, I developed a fear of asking for anything from anyone.

I had this great need for approval and acceptance and because of it, I sometimes made some bad choices. I would avoid any conflict with the fear that someone might not like me. I would do almost anything to be liked. Thank God I was never involved with the wrong crowds and didn't fall into crime or drugs.

I avoided any change in my personal life. I had my routine and I stuck to it. Whenever new people came into our group of friends, I would creep into my shell and hardly spoke to anyone for a couple of hours until I started to relax a bit. Whenever someone asked me what was wrong, I always just said that I was busy acclimatizing. This caused many people to think I was stuck-up and that I did not want to speak to them when in fact, the truth was that I very dearly wanted to. I just didn't know how. The only time this was not a problem was when I had been drinking, and I did not like to always be buzzed to be able to speak to strangers.

It was not until I met my wife that I started to be more confident and believe in myself. She really made me see that I had a lot to offer and should start standing up for myself and what I believed in. For the first time in my life, I started to believe that I had something to offer and that I could achieve everything I wanted.

It was never easy, and I had to go through many hardships and ups and downs, but I have reached a level of self-conviction that I never thought I would have.

I started pursuing my dreams and even other fields that I would have never done before. After a life-changing car accident, I really found myself. It took a lot of soul-searching and tough self-talks to find the real me. I used my circumstances to fuel me instead of becoming a victim of it.

The truth is, we all have our own difficulties that we should deal with, and it is highly likely that nobody else's situation is exactly the same as yours. Regardless, you can still use the same attitudes that others used to find your peace and victory.

This book will not change your circumstances, but it will give you the tools to be able to deal with it and rise above it to become the person you were meant to be.

If you apply the skills and attributes that you learn in this book, it can truly change you forever. One of my greatest mentors, Jim Rohn, used to say, "For things to change you have to change." I can tell you now that this statement is absolutely true.

I first had to change my own self-belief before I could change my situation.

This is how I did it.

Chapter 1

Where It All Started

I grew up in a small mining village in South Africa. I was just a regular boy who loved playing outside. I have always been very adventurous and whenever I saw a tree, a mountain, or a tower, I needed to climb it. I spent a lot of my time playing in the forest by myself. I was the youngest of five children, and because of this all my siblings thought that I was being spoiled, but this was not the case.

In my life, I had to work very hard for everything that I wanted. I never got anything for free, and I worked to get everything that I have.

It is funny how many things that happened in your childhood can have a major effect on your life as an adult. Unfortunately for me, I never realised how deep those scars lie.

Chapter 1   Where It All Started

Many times parents say things that they might not mean to be hurtful, but those words cut deep into the soul of a young child. They may cause you to create a hard outer shell that you hide your inner child inside and many times you never let your inner child out of that shell. You forget about your dreams, plans, passions, and in many cases, your happiness.

Think back to your childhood. Which of you have ever heard these words from your parents?

"Stop that," "Don't be stupid," "Go play," "I'm busy right now," "Don't bother me," "What were you thinking?" "Don't do that," "You are just being silly," "Go play outside, you are bothering me," "Leave that alone," "Don't touch that," "Forget about that, it's just not meant to be," "Ah well, you tried," "I just don't want you to get hurt," "Don't eat so much, you are going to get fat," "If you don't get your act together, you won't amount to anything," "You stupid boy/girl," "If you don't study hard and get good grades, you will never get a good job," "We just weren't meant to be rich."

These are just a few phrases that I am sure many of you have heard throughout your childhood and even worse, some of you might be saying these things to your kids. The sad fact is that the words our parents said directly to us or in our presence has embedded itself into our subconscious. These negative words are now so ingrained into who we are that we have started to believe them as true. This, however, is not a true reflection of the person that you are, but it is just a subconscious belief that was instilled in you by others. So, the same things happened to me in my childhood.

Chapter 1 Where It All Started

Words that were spoken to me or in my presence made me feel negative, inferior, and not good enough. For many years, I believed that I was meant to be mediocre and struggle through life just as my parents did. I did not think that I was ever going to be more than just a worker.

However, I was never happy being just like a fish in a river floating downstream, just going along for the ride. I felt more like a trout and wanted to swim upstream. Deep within me, my inner child was kicking and screaming to let him out of the hard shell that I had locked him in. I felt uncomfortable just staying in a job that I was not passionate about. I have always believed that I was meant to do more, but I didn't know what.

Because of many of the things that happened to me in my childhood, I had very low self-esteem, I avoided conflict, I did not make friends easily, and I spent more time by myself than with friends. After school when I started working, I made a new friend at work. He, in contrast, was a social butterfly and had many friends. He pulled me into his circle of friends and almost overnight, I had many friends. This felt great. We ended up being best friends and spent a lot of time together.

I used to be very lively and friendly when I had a couple of drinks; I felt free and often much more talkative. This also seemed to make other people like me more because they were actually seeing the real me.

Chapter 1   Where It All Started

One night while we were having a party at my friend's house, I met the woman of my dreams. As she came in, our eyes met over a crowded room and my heart skipped a beat. It turns out that the party that I almost did not go to ended up being one of my life-changing moments. We ended up talking for hours and I felt so close to her from the first moment we met. I shared some of my passions and dreams with her, dreams I have never shared with anyone. The best thing was she didn't laugh at my dreams like so many others including my family. She encouraged me and made me believe that I can achieve anything. The same wonderful woman is now my wife and she brings much joy to me.

Shortly after we met, I decided to pursue my dream of becoming a fighter pilot in the air force. My first application to the Air Force was unsuccessful, but I was recruited into the Army to be trained as an ammunition specialist. At first, I didn't want to take the position, but after talking to one of my friends in the Air Force, I decided to take it.

Of course, my parents did not want me to go and my dad in his own words said I was making the biggest mistake of my life. He just used more colorful words than these, though. When my sister found out I was going, she asked me why I wanted to go. I told her that it has been a lifelong dream of mine. She, in turn, told me that I have a messed-up dream. Again, she used more colorful words.

This time I decided not to let my family decide on what I needed to do with my life or make my decisions for me. I was over 21 years of age and could make my own decisions.

Chapter 1   Where It All Started

I decided to take the job and go to the Army. This was another big life-changing event for me.

In the military, they break you down and build you up as a soldier. They teach you how to follow orders, how to lead, how to fight and yes, how to kill, or more importantly, how not to get killed.

The biggest thing that I learned was that no matter how tough it is or how tough it gets, you can make it through. You don't quit and you don't let your buddies quit. I'm still good friends with a few of the guys that were in the Army with me. You build a brother bond that you cannot explain to others. We have suffered together, we have sweated together, we have prayed together, we have cried together, and we have bled together. If you allow it, the experience will make you mentally strong, but for many, it broke them down and they quit. The Defence Force might not be for everybody, but I do believe that it makes you stronger and a better leader for the future.

I eventually got my transfer to go to the Air Force, but I ended up in the Command and Control Department and not pilot training. Unfortunately, due to some of the changes that were happening in our country, pilots were no longer chosen by their ability, but by other political factors, and due to huge budget cuts only a very few ever made it into pilot training. This along with a damaged lung made it impossible for me to become a fighter pilot. However, this did not keep me from still becoming a pilot. Even though I could not become a

Chapter 1   Where It All Started

fighter pilot, I still completed my private pilot's license and spent a few glorious years exploring the skies.

(That's me in the middle)

Chapter 1 Where It All Started

Things may not have turned out exactly the way I planned, but at least I was able to fly, even though it was only for a while. You see, something would happen that would change the course of my life and would force me to become the person I was always meant to be. Your life can change in an instant and plans that you have for your future might not be what is in the cards for you. I always say that God has a reason and purpose for all of us on this planet, and He's trying to nudge you into your ultimate divine purpose. The thing is that for some people a nudge is not enough. Some people need to be pushed, some people need to be bumped, and others need a little harder hit. Now don't get me wrong, God doesn't let the bad things happen in your life, but He always uses it to turn out for your good.

Chapter 1   Where It All Started

You see, throughout my life, many things happened that made me feel that God definitely has a plan for me.

The first thing that made me realise this was when I found out that I was never planned by my parents. You see my father had a vasectomy, but it turns out that the doctor made a mistake, I found my way through impossible odds, and here I am today. The second time I was still a baby. On the evening that I took my first steps, my parents had to rush me to the hospital. I was overcome with almost every lung illness you can have at once and I very nearly died. My mother told me that they prayed for me so much and that an anonymous lady also came to pray for me and that shortly after that my fever broke and I started to get better. Unfortunately, those events left a lasting scar on my lungs, and because of that, one of my lungs is underdeveloped.

There are so many examples I can give right now, but for the purposes of this book, I will only focus on the most recent event that nearly took my life and shook me to the core. This one event had the biggest impact on my life and has set me up for my future success without me even realising it.

Chapter 1   Where It All Started

Chapter 1 Where It All Started

Chapter 2

The Crash That Made Me Move

So, there we were, my beautiful wife and I on our way to a spring dance in the neighboring town called Witbank. We were driving along, talking, laughing, and having a really good time. It was starting to get dark, and the road was very busy. In front of us was a small delivery truck. I believe that the lights of the truck were not working because it was driving with its hazard lights on. As we crossed the bridge our lane split into two, but the lane coming from the front was only a single lane. What I couldn't see happening was that another vehicle was overtaking a truck coming from the front and was coming into our lane. The delivery truck in front of me saw this happening and swerved out of the way. There was no time for me to react and the oncoming vehicle hit me head on, with most of the damage on the right side of the car which was the driver side.

I was unconscious for a while but woke up still sitting in the car. I could hear my wife on the phone trying to get hold of the emergency services. When she couldn't reach them (EMS is not always so good in SA) she phoned my sister who was at the dance we were on our way to. My sister had a friend who was a paramedic and she immediately gave him a call.

Chapter 2   The Crash That Made Me Move

It turns out that he was on duty that night and they were already on the road that our accident was on heading back from another accident towards the hospital. My sister informed them that we were also in an accident on that road and that they needed to turn around and go back.

By the time the paramedics came to the accident site I was barely breathing, and if they had to come from the hospital they would have been too late to save me. This in itself was a miracle. They had to drain my lungs of fluids on the scene and closed up one of the open fractures on my right elbow.

When we got to the hospital it was a frantic rush to get me stabilized. My lungs wanted to collapse, my liver and kidneys were badly damaged, and I had some internal bleeding. The bleeding miraculously stopped by itself to the astonishment of the doctors. After about three hours of constant struggling, I was finally stable enough to be moved into a room.

I had a crushed right elbow, damaged right shoulder, torn right hamstring, damaged right hip, whiplash, and my kidneys, liver, and other internal organs including my lungs were damaged. My left kneecap was shattered and the tendon holding it was torn from my lower leg.

Chapter 2   The Crash That Made Me Move

Chapter 2   The Crash That Made Me Move

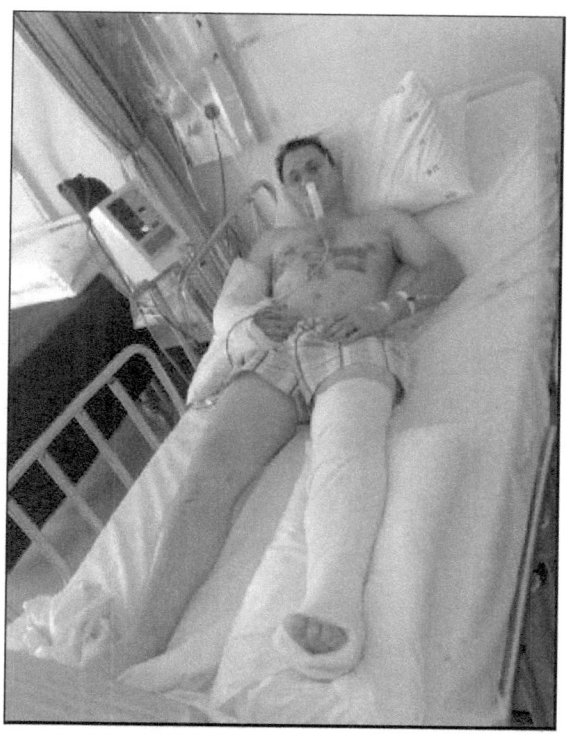

The accident happened on a Friday night and due to my injuries, I was only stable enough to be operated on the following Wednesday. I must admit that I have never felt pain like I felt directly after the operation. Ten days after the accident I walked out of the hospital. With a lot of effort and a lot of pain, I made my way to the car and I had to lie down on the backseat because I could not sit in the front due to my leg not being able to bend.

Chapter 2   The Crash That Made Me Move

About three days after leaving the hospital my right arm started to drain from the wound so I went to my doctor. The wound had become infected and because of the severe impact caused by the accident on my elbow, the stitches were opening up and couldn't keep the wound closed anymore. To try to counter the infection they gave me antibiotics and I had to wear a vacuum pump to suck the draining fluids out of the wound to try to close the wound. Eventually I ended up having to wear the vacuum pump for four months. My body eventually started to become allergic to the plasters that they used and started to reject it. I would get blisters on my skin and when they would pull off the plaster, my skin would come off with it. They would then clean my arm, apply iodine, and then reapply the plasters for the vacuum pump. This was a horrifying experience and I hated having to wear a vacuum pump. Because of the infection, the bone in my elbow didn't want to fuse properly and it took eight months after the accident to be fused enough for the doctors to be able to remove the stainless-steel pins that were installed in my elbow.

During this period the small bone fragments that were inside my elbow moved into the joint and started growing there, forcing out the cartilage and fusing the ulna and the humerus bones together. Because of this, I have lost all movement in my right elbow. This, in turn, led to a lot of frustration. I used to be very independent and being placed in a vulnerable position where I had to rely on other people to assist me with some of my basic needs was very hard in the beginning. I had

Chapter 2   The Crash That Made Me Move

to learn to do many things with my left hand. I had to learn to eat with my left hand, brush teeth with my left, fix my hair with my left hand and basically do everything else with my left hand. This was very difficult for me and I turned into a grumpy and unpleasant person.

One day my wife came to me and said that she didn't know how to act around me anymore because I had become withdrawn and sometimes very grumpy. I realised that I had a choice: I could either sit and sulk or I could get up and go on with my life. Not being able to use my elbow is not a life sentence and I realised that there are so many other people all way worse off than I am and they still enjoy an amazing life. Just type in 'inspirational people living with disabilities' in any internet browser and see what comes up.

I realised that I could take what happened to me and use it to strengthen me and to help others by making a difference in the world.

"It's not what happens to you,
but how you react to it that matters."
Epictetus

Chapter 2   The Crash That Made Me Move

There are many things that happen to us during our lives. Things we have no control over. What we do, however, have control over is how it affects us. We have the choice to how we will respond to what has happened to us. I have realised over time that there is one absolute certainty, and that is choice. We don't have a choice about what happens to us, but we do have a choice about what happens within us. What I mean with this is that anything that happens in your life has the ability to turn you into a better person, a stronger person, but the choice is up to you.

I had to make that choice for myself. No one else could make it for me. I decided that no matter what happens to me I will not let it get me down. I started looking for opportunities and I started doing more than was expected from me. According to my employer, I was deemed unfit for work as a boilermaker, which was my profession at the time of the accident. Even though this was a hard blow because I was just 28 years old at the time, I did not let it keep me down. I decided to look for places where I could learn new skills in the same company. I started asking the planner questions about his job. I asked him what I could do to help him to make his job easier. In turn, he suggested that while I could not do my former job I could be trained as a planner successor. I grabbed the opportunity and I learned as much as I could as quickly as I could. During this process, my efforts were recognized by the procurement manager and I was offered a job as a buyer with the same company.

Chapter 2 The Crash That Made Me Move

The fact that I had taken the time and effort to learn the systems that the company was using meant that I was a perfect candidate for the position, and if I had not gone out on my own to learn more and to study the systems, then I would not have been given the opportunity.

It had turned out that what I believed to be one of the worst things in my life, God intended for my benefit. I was suddenly in a new job where I could learn new skills and I was earning more money than before the accident.

Because I was given the opportunity to work as a buyer, I decided to give it my everything. I again jumped into my work and I focused on learning as much as possible as quickly as possible. Within a very short space of time, I was working as a full-time buyer without any assistance. I handled all the different types of commodities and as I mastered one they gave me the next one. Before the end of that first year, I had moved up to a position where I handled imports and projects. This was a senior position for a person that had only been in the department for less than a year. Not only that, but I was also the youngest to achieve this position at the time.

You see, it is easy to sit and complain about what happened to you, and nobody will deny that whatever has happened to you was indeed a big deal, but you do not have to let that determine what the rest of your life is going to look like. And don't let something that happened to you externally destroy what is going on internally. You have something to give,

Chapter 2   The Crash That Made Me Move

something you can offer the world in a way that no one else can. Make the choice to be the best you can be, to use what has happened to you to your benefit and to the benefit of others.

> *"Your attitude, not your aptitude,*
> *will determine your altitude."*
> *Zig Ziglar*

If I look back now at the times that I felt very low and down, I realised that it would have been very easy for me to stay there, to let them declare me medically unfit for work, and go on disability pension. I could have sat there complaining and crying about why it happened to me, but that would not have benefitted me in any way. I had every right to be upset because the person that caused the accident had been drinking, he overtook on a solid white line, and he caused a terrible accident. Unfortunately, he paid for his mistake with his life. I would always get so upset when people heard that he had died; they would say that it was good because he caused the accident. I would then, in turn, say to them that nobody deserves to die in that way and that he had made a mistake, but it is not our place to judge him. Many times, people do stupid things that cause harm to others, and many times the people doing the things that can harm others are ourselves. We hurt others not only with our actions but also with our words.

Chapter 2   The Crash That Made Me Move

Our words are one of the most powerful weapons that we have, and we use them every day so negligently that we don't even give a second thought as to what we are saying to others, and more importantly, to ourselves. We should be more careful about what we say to ourselves and about ourselves. Remember that your subconscious mind is always listening to what you're saying, and if you are saying negative and bad things about yourself, how can you expect your life to be positive and fulfilling? Start giving yourself a little bit of credit. If you do something good, congratulate yourself and celebrate. Start loving yourself so that you can love others. Accept yourself and accept your shortcomings because only then will you be able to work on them, improve, and become a better person.

You might be wondering what that has to do with getting over an accident or a divorce or an illness. The answer is that it's got everything to do with it because the way you talk to yourself subconsciously determines your behavior towards the situation. If you were negative about the situation, then that situation seems even worse than it actually is. If you are positive about the situation, then you see things better than they are and you tend to see the potential in the situation. You see how you can use things that happen to you to make you stronger. Don't complain when something happens to you. Accept it, grab it with both hands, and wrestle with it until you find what is good and positive in that situation.

Chapter 2   The Crash That Made Me Move

There are so many stories about people who went through the most difficult times in their lives and came out incredibly successful. These people took these difficult moments in their lives, and instead of letting it hold them back, they used it to strengthen them. Oprah Winfrey, who, after having a very abusive childhood, now is one of the most successful women in the world. Nick Vujicic from Australia, who was born without arms or legs, is making a huge difference in the world. Donald Trump and various other millionaires who went bankrupt were millionaires again within a couple of years. Just because something bad happens to you does not mean that it's the end; it means it's the beginning. A new beginning.

"I encourage you to accept that you may not be able to see a path right now, but that doesn't mean it's not there."

Nick Vujicic

Look for opportunities where you can make a difference. Look for people that are going through the same thing as you are going through right now. Find someone you can talk to, someone who can motivate you and lift you out of despair. Don't lose your faith! God has a plan for your life, and He is preparing you for your divine purpose in this world.

Chapter 2   The Crash That Made Me Move

Barbara De Angelis talks about the divine discomfort, which means that you have a reason you are here, but you don't know what it is yet. You only know that you're uncomfortable with where you are, but you don't know how to change it yet. She compares it to a woman giving birth to a baby. The last couple of weeks just before she gives birth she is uncomfortable. This is similar to you giving birth to yourself, giving birth to the you that you were meant to be.

The best advice I can give you right now is to get comfortable with feeling uncomfortable. When you're feeling uncomfortable, you always look at how you can change things, but when you are comfortable, you tend to stay where you are no matter how unhappy you are.

The first way to go through difficult times is to remain positive.

"The journey in between what you once were and who you are now becoming is where the dance of life takes place."

Barbara De Angelis

Chapter 2   The Crash That Made Me Move

Chapter 2   The Crash That Made Me Move

Chapter 3

Finding Yourself

The journey to a more confident you, free from the constraints of a comfort zone, starts with self-exploration. As I mentioned earlier, I always had a huge passion for aviation and my biggest dream was to become a fighter jet pilot in the South African Air Force. However, after several applications, I was still not accepted and had to look for something else.

While I was still in high school, I had the opportunity to apply for an apprenticeship at a large steel mill in my hometown and was offered a position as a boilermaker apprentice. This was never something I saw myself doing as a career while I was growing up, but it was a great opportunity and I accepted the position. Not many people get jobs directly out of school and I was very grateful for the opportunity.

Life as an apprentice was very exciting because most of us still lived with our parents and suddenly got a salary every month. Needless to say most of my money was spent on partying and not much else, except for my car that I bought. That was my very first big purchase and I was so happy to have my very own brand new car that I was paying for myself.

Chapter 3   Finding Yourself

The best thing that happened to me was meeting my wonderful wife, as mentioned earlier.

That was where my transformation began. I remembered how badly I wanted to become a fighter pilot and I decided that I would do whatever it took to get there.

At that stage, I had just qualified as a Boilermaker Artisan and was appointed as a Plant Maintenance Boilermaker in the same company where I did my apprenticeship and got quite a good salary. I started asking around about people who used to be in the Air Force and one of my colleagues told me about a friend he had in the Air Force. We went to see his friend who was a Sergeant Major working in the Command and Control section of the Air Force. The Sergeant Major told me of a shortage of command post assistants in the Air Force and I knew that this could be my way in, so I applied through the Central Applications Office of the Defence Force.

About a month later, I received a telegram informing me that I was invited for a screening that involved a medical test, psychometric tests, and a full interview in front of a defence board.

This scared me tremendously as this was the first time I felt like I might have to leave my current job. At first, I did not want to go, but after speaking with my wife, who was still my girlfriend at that time, she made me realise how much I wanted to go and that I would have regretted it all my life if I did not go.

Chapter 3 Finding Yourself

When I finally made it to the screening process, I found out that I was selected to become part of a small elite sector in the Army as an ammunition specialist. I was crushed and flattered at the same time. I thought that it was a screening for the air force pilot programme, but it wasn't. Another thing that bugged me was the fact that the training school was almost 900 kilometres from my hometown and my girlfriend, and I would have had to be there for at least four years.

I went back to the sergeant major in the air force and he assured me that I could get a transfer from the army to the air force once I completed my basic military training.

This was a very tough time for me. Should I go and leave behind everything I knew and loved or should I stay in my comfort zone, remain a Boilermaker artisan, and get married and have kids like everyone else?

After a lot of soul-searching and support from my girlfriend, I decided to take the leap of faith and go for it.

The defence force has a unique training philosophy where they break you down completely and build you up into the person and soldier they want you to be. They teach teamwork, honour, and respect, virtues that I believe we should all learn to live by.

I can tell you that it was not easy, and it was not meant to be easy. It is supposed to be tough and challenging and make you a stronger person so that when you get to real combat

Chapter 3   Finding Yourself

you won't freak out. It was one of the toughest times in my life and some of the best times in my life. You learn to hold on to the good times. You learn to pull together as a unit. You learn how to be a big brother to your fellow soldiers. I can tell you that the friends I made there are some of the closest friends I've ever had, and I am still very close to some of them many years later.

I finally got my transfer to the air force, but not without a struggle. The colonel from the ammunition core did not want me to go and wanted me to stay in the ammunition core. After a personal meeting with him, where I discussed my passion and dream for aviation, he decided to let me go.

I was so happy to be in the air force. I worked in the radar sector and command post. Finally, I was working with aircraft, even though I could not see them except on a radar screen. I applied for the pilot training programme and was denied a couple of times due to budget cuts. I got in contact with the commanding officer in charge of pilot recruiting and was told that my chances to become a pilot in the air force were basically zero. This almost shattered my dream, but I figured that I would then become a pilot on my own in the private sector.

I realised that I could not afford training to become a pilot on a military salary as I was earning less than one-fifth of what I was earning as a boilermaker. I then decided to go back to my boilermaker trade in order to raise the money to be able to learn to fly.

Chapter 3   Finding Yourself

My passion for aviation pushed me to find a way to learn to fly no matter how tough it might be. I finally got my private pilot's licence a few years later and started my journey to flying a fighter plane. It might not be in the air force, but I will still do it one day.

Similar to my story that you have just heard, you might also be going through challenging times. But the key is not to let the challenging times keep you from your dream. You need to pursue it no matter what. Your dream needs to be a burning desire within that nothing can keep you from achieving it. Only then will you be able to pursue your dreams even through the tough times. If you can learn how to chase your dreams through the toughest of challenges, it will serve you well throughout your life.

It is important to find what drives you, what you dream of, or what you would like to achieve. You hear so many times about goal setting, but this is not only about goal setting, it is about finding the reason why you want to achieve your goals and dreams.

Jim Rohn also said that if your why is big enough, the how is easy. This does not mean it will be easy to reach your goals, but it does mean that you will find any way possible to make your dreams come true, and if there is no way yet, you will make a way.

I go back many times and think about when I was still a small child playing in the forest by myself. It was some of the

Chapter 3 Finding Yourself

happiest times of my life. I felt free and had such a great imagination. Every day was a blessing and I could make of that day whatever I wanted. No hesitation and no fear. I had to go back in my mind to find that brave, fearless adventurer from my childhood who believed he could achieve anything and let him out again.

You, too, have to find your happiest childhood moment and remember what it felt like to imagine anything you wanted and use that for your future. Look to your future with the knowledge that you can achieve anything you want and that you will make a way to achieve your goals.

Never let anybody tell you it can't be done. Many years ago, it was believed to be impossible to fly, but look at aviation today. Nothing is impossible! With the right mindset and persistence, anything can be made a reality. It is just a matter of time.

Do not let go of your creativity, use it. Let it guide you to find new things and find your true passion. Once you have found that, only then can you start creating your ultimate dream life. Let go of the fear of failure; failure helps us grow. When you were learning how to walk you fell down hundreds of times, but you never gave up and now you are walking. Imagine if you were afraid of falling and decided never to try to walk. Imagine what it would have felt like to see everybody running and playing and knowing you could have done the same thing if only you tried.

Chapter 3   Finding Yourself

Go into your deepest locked away memories, find your childhood dreams, and start working on making them a reality. Never ever let anybody tell you that your dream is silly. The reason many people try to discourage you is because they never had the courage to pursue their dreams, and they don't want you to succeed in the fear that it will make them look bad.

The second way to finding yourself and your purpose starts with learning from every situation.

Never quit learning. The way you grow through challenges will help you achieve your goals much easier in the future.

You can do whatever your heart desires!

Chapter 3   Finding Yourself

Chapter 4

The Challenge of Networking

As comfortable as your comfort zone may be, it is imperative that you try things that make you uncomfortable if you want to grow. As I mentioned before, I used to be very shy and because of this, there were two things I always said. Number one, I will never do public speaking. Number two, I will never do sales. This was not because I did not want to do these things, but because I wanted to and I was afraid to even try. After my car accident, when I was told I would not be able to continue with my career as planned, I had a really hard choice to make. Was I going to change or stay the same?

I realised that if I wanted to grow as a person, then I needed to overcome my fear of speaking to strangers. I got involved with a network marketing company; the name 'network marketing' in itself says that networking is an integral part of the business.

I knew that if I wanted to succeed in the business, I needed to learn how to network like a professional.

Chapter 4   The Challenge of Networking

My first opportunity to start networking was when one of my wife's friends invited me to a networking opportunity with the local BNI (Business Network International) chapter. At the very first meeting, I was in a situation where I needed to talk to people I did not know. In essence, BNI is an organisation where businesses refer business to each other.

As I started attending the local events, what they called business buzz events, I slowly started to make a little bit of progress towards becoming better at networking. At first, I would just stand on my own, not really knowing anybody and not knowing how to make contact with people. I would just stand there with the silly smile on my face hoping that somebody else would start talking to me. This might sound silly to you, but that is exactly how I used to be. You can just imagine the image of this shy guy standing in a room full of people with his hands in his pockets, just shyly looking around and smiling at everybody that looked his way, hoping that somebody would choose to talk to him.

Luckily for me, most of these events were attended by more or less the same people. So, as time went on I started to know these people, and even became friends with them. This helped me with future networking events to feel like part of the inner circle. I then began to look for new people at the events and then introduce them to the people that I already knew. Pretty soon, I became a connector of people. I started to feel like I belonged, and that people trusted and respected me.

Chapter 4   The Challenge of Networking

As I got better and better at networking, I started to go to different events, bigger events, and even went to networking opportunities in the Johannesburg, which was a much bigger city than my small hometown. I started to realise that I was really good at making contact with people and really connecting with them on a one-on-one level. I started to enjoy networking. This led to me getting involved with the local chamber of commerce and industry where I later became an executive member.

If you really want to get out of your comfort zone, you need to learn how to network. Networking is not simply people meeting each other and sticking business cards in each other's hands. Networking is about building relationships, about truly connecting with people and seeing how you can help them solve problems. You might not be able to help them personally, but you might know somebody that will be able to help them. You then become the connector that connects them with somebody that can help them solve a problem. This helps you to create credibility and earn respect.

Once you have earned the respect of the people around you, they will be much more likely to refer business to you and to trust you with their contacts.

I know that it might seem like a daunting task to think that you need to start networking with people that you do not know, but I would like to tell you that you were not born to hide away. You were born to shine.

Chapter 4 The Challenge of Networking

The biggest reason why people do not like networking is because of what they think others might think of them. They are afraid that people will think they are not good enough, that they are silly, or that they just plain don't belong. I can tell you now that you are more than capable of networking in any room with any person from any company. All you need to do is overcome your fear of what other people might be thinking of you. One way to do this is to realise that you do have something to offer the world. There is something inside of you that no man had to teach you, something that you are good at with which you can add value to other people's lives.

Romans 8:31 says that if God is for us, who can be against us? He who did not spare His own son, but gave Him up for us all – how will He not also, along with His son, Jesus, graciously give all things?

We do not need to be afraid of anything. Fear is something that we are imagining that has not yet happened and is not real. The only thing that gives fear strength is our beliefs. The way you think about yourself will always reflect your circumstances.

Proverbs 23:7 "For as a man thinketh in his heart, so is he!"

This in itself proves that the way that you think defines who you are and will also manifest itself in your current reality. You need to believe in yourself, and only when you start believing in yourself will you realise that other people can also believe in you.

Chapter 4   The Challenge of Networking

Denis Waitley said that when he wrote his first book it lay in his drawer for a very long time, and it wasn't because the book wasn't any good, but because the author was not (or he believed he wasn't).

As soon as he started to believe in himself and in his own abilities, only then could he see the value in what he wrote in his book and get it published. But, until he believed it, it could not happen.

So, one of the keys to good networking is in realising that you do have value to offer. You have the ability in you to solve problems for people. It does not matter where you come from, what your background is, or what your experience is at this very moment. There are people out there that are looking for the exact skills that you have this very moment. Your job is to make yourself available for them to find you. That will not happen if you sit at home and hide away. Be bold!

People were not meant to be alone, so don't hide from people. You just need to learn how to make friends.

The fastest way for you to learn how to network is to start. Look for networking opportunities in your area and tie into them. Network as often as you can, wherever you can. At first, it will be a little bit scary and you will not be very good at it, but as you do it more often you will get better and better each time. The key is to start.

Chapter 4 The Challenge of Networking

Don't wait for anybody else to do it for you because they won't. You need to do it for yourself and you need to start right now.

A great way to start is to join a network marketing company. This is a very good environment to learn because you are constantly amongst people that want to help you succeed. This has truly helped me and started me on my way to becoming the person I am today.

"For things to change, you have to change"

Jim Rohn

During the time I was working as a buyer, I always kept my eyes open for new opportunities. My brother-in-law had lost his job and had been staying with us. He was also looking for new opportunities and came across a network marketing company. He was invited to go to a meeting at a gentleman's house about one hundred and fifty kilometers away. Since he did not have a vehicle, he asked me if I could take him to the meeting. I took him to the meeting and while I was there, I really liked what I saw, so I decided to also join this multi-level marketing company. People that do not understand multi-level marketing companies normally give them a bad rap. My experience, however, is that it is one of the best

Chapter 4   The Challenge of Networking

business opportunities in which you can learn the most about business and yourself for the least amount of financial outlay possible.

As a gift for our commitment, our upline in the company gave us each a set of Jim Rohn's 2004 weekend event audio discs. This was the beginning of the change for me. It was the very first time that I came across motivational speakers and motivators that truly spoke to the soul. In those CDs I found a glimmer of hope that I, too, could one day be a public speaker, even though I had always been afraid of speaking in front of any number of people.

Some of the people that spoke at that event were Jim Rohn, Denis Waitley, Brian Tracy, Vic Johnson, Chris Widener, and Donna Krech to name but a few. The words of immense wisdom that I got out of a couple of CDs made me realise that every single one of us has exactly the same opportunities and exactly the same possibilities of being successful. I realised that the choice to be successful lay within me, and that by listening to these wise teachers, following their teachings, and applying them to my life, I could become great and successful.

"Success begins when your actions become greater than your excuses."

Mike Rodriguez

Chapter 4   The Challenge of Networking

Now the road to the top is never easy and I had many challenges along the way. I started my business being shy, afraid of talking to people that I didn't know, and had the fear of failure pulling me back all the time. But, by starting slowly and with belief in the product, I started to build my customer base. I realised that the biggest thing that was holding me back all my life was not my background or where I was at that moment, it was my belief that I was not good enough and my fear of failure. All these beliefs stemmed out of my childhood, but I never realised it.

I started going to every single training the company offered to learn from the successful people in the company. Many times, I drove 300 kilometers every weekend to attend the big trainings that they had in the city. I was like a hungry wolf that was chasing after its prey; I was not going to let it go because I wanted to find myself and my success. I learned a little bit more every week, and pretty soon, I was asked to assist in the training by performing a small part of the process. The beautiful thing about the multi-level marketing company is that you always get a lot of praise. No matter how scared I was, they kept motivating me and making me believe that I was doing a good job, and that was awesome.

I found myself loving being in front of the audience and pretty soon, I started to volunteer to do some of the training. Little by little, they gave me more and more responsibility and eventually I was asked to do a retail training.

Chapter 4   The Challenge of Networking

"The essence of influence is pull. It's an attraction. Great influencers attract people, to themselves, and to their ideas."

Bob Burg

That was just the beginning for me. I found myself looking for more and more opportunities to be able to talk to others and share my story because what I found was that a successful story spoke to the hearts of the people. And without heart, you've got no connection and if you don't have a connection with your customers, you don't have a business.

I have since bought many audiobooks from authors like Jim Rohn, Brian Tracy, Robin Sharma, Dave Ramsey, Zig Ziglar, Norman Vincent Peale, and many more. These books helped me become a better person by allowing me to find my inner strength and courage to go out and do more, work harder, and help more people.

I also believe that when you are ready, God opens doors for you. Because I was ready and I was looking for a place where I can give my best, I also found numerous other networking opportunities. This was brilliant not only for business, but also for my self-esteem. I got involved with multiple organizations and after just a couple of months, I was asked to become the educational coordinator for a group of business people in the local BNI chapter. This was a huge honor for me and since then, I have spoken to between 25 and 40 business owners every week.

Chapter 4   The Challenge of Networking

"Doubt kills more dreams than failure ever will."
Suzy Kassem

I also became part of our local chamber of commerce and went to every networking opportunity that I could find. I had met many new friends and through that, I had been able to motivate many people. I was asked to be part of a modelling competition as one of the sponsors and one of the judges. This has given my business a lot of free marketing and visibility in the community. I believe that it is important to be well-known in your community as someone that makes a difference and has a kind heart.

Another life-changing event for me was when my wife and I went to the first Millionaire Mind Intensive that was held in South Africa. The reason I say that that was a life-changing event for me is because at the event they really go deep into your subconscious mind and uncover your hidden thoughts and feelings about things like rich people, being wealthy, and being successful. I discovered many of the issues that I kept inside myself since childhood that were holding me back, many of which shocked me deeply. I have never spent so much time crying at an event than I did at that Millionaire Mind Intensive. The beautiful thing was that my wife was there with me, and both of us walked out of that event completely different people. Due to the massive results that we had seen from that one event, we decided to sign up for other courses that were coming to South Africa.

Chapter 4   The Challenge of Networking

This turned out to be the biggest investment in my self-development that I have ever made, and it was worth it. The next event was a business training session where I learned more about business in one weekend than in my entire working life before the event. My wife and I walked out of the event so fired up with new ideas of how we want to do business and things we wanted to achieve. We promised ourselves that no matter what, we would keep that positive energy and positive mindset and not allow other people to drag us down. At first, it was a little difficult because one tends to slip back into old habits. Luckily, because both of us attended the training, we supported each other and motivated each other to keep going.

I'm telling you now that it is much easier to make the changes you need to make in your life if you have someone there with you and supporting you. Find yourself an accountability partner that will keep your feet to the fire and that will keep you motivated and going when times get tough. When you're in the seminar and you are around hundreds of other positive people, it's very easy to be positive yourself, but the big challenge comes when you leave the seminar and you get back into the real world with people bombarding you with negativity and challenges around every corner, that's when you need to be strong. That is when you need to stay focused, remember what you learned during the seminar, and apply it to your life.

Many of us spent lots of time listening to motivational

Chapter 4   The Challenge of Networking

speakers, going through training programs, and attending seminars, but very few of us actually apply what we've learned. If you do not apply what you learn in the seminars, then they are just expensive entertainment. But, if you apply what you've learned and you make a conscious effort to implement every single thing you learn to make your business and your life better, then it's a valuable investment that will pay you back hundreds of times over.

It is not always easy to remember everything you learned during the seminar or to apply it all to your business, but if you start small and implement the little things, then big changes can happen overnight.

Never stop networking, because you will get better every time.

Come on, get out there and make a difference!

I look forward to seeing you at a networking event someday.

Chapter 4 The Challenge of Networking

Chapter 4 The Challenge of Networking

Chapter 5

Procrastination: The Dream Killer

Procrastination has killed more dreams than we could ever really fathom. To find your way out of the zone, you need to learn to fight against it. Just think about how many times you heard someone, when getting close to what they believed is the end of their life, say that they wish they would have done this or that. People think there is still lots of time while they are still young, and before you know it, most of your life has passed you by. However, old age is not a reason not to follow your dream. Take the founder of one of the world's most famous fried chicken brands. He started franchising his chicken recipe very late in his life and to this day, it is still the biggest thing that he is known for.

I can remember when I was a young apprentice our town was rapidly expanding into a city. I always had an eye for potential and there was a specific point where two roads met that I believed would have been the ideal place for a fast food drive-through restaurant. I would constantly tell my friends that we should open a fast food restaurant there, but due to a lack of knowledge and understanding of how business works, I never did it. And a few years later, the exact same restaurant that I

Chapter 5   Procrastination: The Dream Killer

wanted to build there was built and it was a huge success, even to this day.

You see, it is easy for me to say I couldn't afford it, or I didn't have the knowhow, or even that I was too young. But the truth of the matter is that if I was serious about pursuing that dream, then I would have found a way to make it happen. I would have found someone to mentor me and guide me through the process. Now some people might say, "What if that person stole your idea?" Believe me, I know all of the excuses, and that is all that they are. A lot of those people that you share your idea with are just as clueless as you and even more afraid of trying than you. If you keep looking, you will find a sincere individual who would be willing to help you if you show true commitment. Even if you have to give away a share of your company to get them involved, it is still worth it.

As I touched on in the previous paragraph, fear is a big reason many people don't follow their dreams. I know, because it has kept me from pursuing many of my own dreams, and sometimes when my dreams are big enough, I still feel fear trying to move back in. One of the most profound explanations of fear that I could find, I heard in the movie, **After Earth**. The gentleman said, *"Fear is not real! It is your mind playing tricks on you based on a reality that does not yet exist."* This was quite profound to me. I realised that fear can be a very powerful, protective instinct when you use it to protect your life, but fear should never be debilitating. We imagine

Chapter 5   Procrastination: The Dream Killer

scenarios playing out in our heads that haven't even happened yet, and based on those scenarios we manifest fearful beliefs and that keeps us from acting. Once we realise that there are just as many positive outcomes as negative ones, then we can choose to focus on the positives, and oftentimes that is exactly what we will get.

The biggest of these fears is the fear of failing. We tend to be so preoccupied about what people might say or think if we try and fail. We are so afraid of losing everything. Well, if you look at Job in the Bible, losing everything might not be so bad because God might have something much bigger and better planned for you. Job was a very rich man with abundant livestock and a loving family. He eventually lost everything. Even his friends started to attack him emotionally. Job remained loyal to God and he kept on working hard, and regardless of being physically ill at the time, he kept believing and trusting God, and ultimately, he ended up with much more than he had lost. God can use your difficulties and trials as a lesson to others.

Dictionary.com defines Failure as "an act or instance of failing or proving unsuccessful; lack of success" This means that, as Zig Ziglar used to say, "Failure is an event, not a person." Failure also means lack of success, which could be linked to time. At a specific space in time, there might be a lack of success, but that does not mean that there will always be a lack of success. If you keep going, and keep learning, and trying, then eventually you will be successful. It is a law of

Chapter 5   Procrastination: The Dream Killer

nature. There is absolutely no way that you can keep growing, learning, and getting better, and never achieve success. Ultimately, you just have to succeed, and you will.

Failure is only permanent if you accept it and if you don't learn anything from it. Never let it define you, but let it inspire you.

There are many time-wasters out there that also keep us from achieving our goals and dreams. One of the biggest ones is television. Many people spend hours a day watching television. I used to spend many hours a day in front of the TV and over weekends when there was a sport on, I would spend almost the entire weekend in front of the TV. This stole so much of my time and I never got anything done. I would always complain that I didn't have enough time to do the things I needed to do, when the fact is, that I had more than enough time; I was wasting it on the wrong things. If you get home at 5:30 PM and watch TV until 10:00 PM before going to bed, that equates to 22.5 hours of TV in 5 days.

Let's assume you spend from about 1:00 PM to 10:00 PM watching TV on Saturdays and Sundays. That brings your weekly total to a staggering 40.5 hours. Let's say you earn an average of $20 per hour. That then equates to $810 per week, which means that your TV costs you about $42,120 per year. Shocking, right? This is time you can be spending on creating more money rather than allowing your TV to steal it from you.

Chapter 5   Procrastination: The Dream Killer

Another distraction that might be becoming even bigger than TV, especially today and with younger generations, is social media. People spend an inordinate amount of time looking at other people's fake lives while they should be living their own. We get lost scrolling from one post to the next not realising how much time we spend browsing through other people's lives.

If you ever want to become successful, you need to get away from the things that steal your productive time and start focusing on the things that you need to do to get you closer to your dreams and goals. Now there are people who are extremely passionate about social media and they make a decent living from it, but if you are not making any money from it, or learning anything from it, then you are wasting your time.

Now, you should also not fall into the trap of telling yourself that you are learning and spending most of your time learning new things and hence social media is not time wasting. Well, it is, if you are not going to use what you are learning right now to get you to your goals. It reminds me of a lady's testimony at one of the training seminars of the network marketing companies I was in. She said that when she joined the company, she spent days working on the perfect flyer and layout for her business cards. She wanted it to be perfect. This kept her from getting out there amongst the potential customers and actually earning some money. There is an important lesson we can learn from this woman. Don't waste

Chapter 5 Procrastination: The Dream Killer

your time creating the perfect flyer. Just start and get better and better every day as you grow.

Friends and family can be masters at causing you to procrastinate. They do this by enticing you with all sorts of social events that keep you from working on achieving your goals. That is why one of the most difficult areas that you need to work on while chasing your dreams and getting out of your comfort zone is to have a close look at the people you spend most of your time with. Many people won't understand why you want to change who you are or what you do, and due to this, they will try to hold you back. It might not always be a conscious thing on their part, but it is damaging to your progress nonetheless. When you are being attacked by friends or family, their words tend to stick, and you find yourself starting to believe what they are saying is true and this will aggravate the procrastination habit. People, especially family, will say that they are trying to protect you. This might be true, but remember that the whole world thought that the Wright brothers were crazy and were going to kill themselves. However, when they took their historic flight at Kitty Hawk in North Carolina on December 17th, 1903, something amazing happened. Even though their first flight lasted only 12 seconds and only covered 120 feet, they proved the concept and aviation as a viable form of transport was born. Because of their commitment, we can now travel to almost anywhere in the world in a single day.

Find someone that will help you, that will motivate you, and inspire you to become even more and better.

Chapter 5   Procrastination: The Dream Killer

Many friends will not understand when you start spending less time with them. This does not mean that they are not still good friends, but just that you are focusing on growing into a new person. Don't allow them to guilt you into spending more time with them and not on pursuing your dream. This can be a difficult form of procrastination to shake off due to the fact that other people's emotions are involved, but stay strong. You can't change who you are by staying in the same circumstances. You need to get a new perspective.

Find people that have already achieved what you would like to achieve, or something similar, and spend time with them. Ask them questions, listen to their conversations, and ask them to help you. You can learn more from people like that than you could ever learn from a university degree.

I had an opportunity to spend time with a multi-millionaire and a billionaire one weekend and I listened intently while they spoke. The amount of life experience and knowledge they had was just mind blowing. I learned so much from them in a couple of hours and I still apply those lessons today, along with some other valuable ones I picked up along the way.

So, have a close look at your family and friends you spend most of your time with. You don't necessarily have to end friendships unless they are directly sabotaging your progress, but limit the time you spend with negative people while you grow, and maybe in the future, if they are willing, they can learn from you.

Chapter 5   Procrastination: The Dream Killer

Remember that time is the great equaliser, and that everyone has twenty-four hours a day. How you spend those hours will determine your results. The only difference between you and a multi-millionaire is what you spend your time on. Remember to use those twenty-four hours wisely.

"You become the average of the five people you spend the most time with."
Jim Rohn

Chapter 5   Procrastination: The Dream Killer

Chapter 5   Procrastination: The Dream Killer

Chapter 6

Believe in Yourself

Believing in yourself is one of the most important aspects of achieving success. The road that leads out of the zone is paved with self-belief. If you think about it, for anything in life, you first need to believe that you can do it before you can do it. It is like running the 100-meter hurdles. You never know if you can do it or not until you see someone do it and think to yourself, "I can do that." Then, you go and try it until you perfect it.

The point is that there must first be some belief that you can do it for you to be willing to attempt it, and once you have tried it the first time, you learn a little more technique and you develop yourself into the best you can possibly be.

If I never believed that I could become a pilot and fly someday, then I would have never pursued it in the first place and probably would have never become a pilot, or a speaker, or an author, or an international property investor, or any of the other things that have stemmed from my willingness to pursue my dreams.

Chapter 6   Believe in Yourself

I now know that the reason I wanted to become a fighter pilot was not to go to war and drop bombs. It was to get the freedom I believed that flying would bring me, flying low to the ground at the speed of sound seeing everything flash by so quickly. That is what I wanted. The truth is, even if I did manage to become a fighter pilot in the air force, it still would not have made me happy if I was not happy with where I was within myself.

I needed to stop seeing myself as worthless and needed to start being the person I wanted to be. I needed to stop my negative self-talk and start building myself up with my words and my thoughts.

To reach your ultimate level of success you first need to start believing in yourself.

Sometimes this is easier said than done, especially if you have such low self-esteem as I used to have. After years of people telling you that you are a loser and that you will amount to nothing, it is quite difficult to start believing something different.

No matter what you do in life, if you are not happy with yourself, nothing will truly make you happy. It's the same with love; you can't truly love someone else until you learn to love yourself. At some point in my life, I thought that if I could only make everybody else around me happy then I would be happy. It does not work like that! Don't look to others for your happiness, create your own.

Chapter 6   Believe in Yourself

For me, it was a matter of building up the courage to let myself wander out of my comfort zone a little bit at a time. The more I did it, the easier it became, and pretty soon I was doing things I never thought I would.

I started by trying small things that I did not know how to do, and I tried it until I could do it. An example of this was buying my very first computer in 2002. At that stage, I knew nothing about how computers worked. I got my computer, started working on it a little at a time, and started asking others to help me. My girlfriend knew a lot about computers and she helped me immensely in the beginning. In no time at all, I could do almost anything I wanted to on a computer and whenever we had computer issues, my girlfriend would ask me to fix it because I had so much patience.

I kept finding small things and developing myself until I could do it properly.

Also, note that I say that I developed myself until I could do it because the fact is that you cannot change that task, but you can learn how to do it.

Any skill in the world today is learnable if you are willing to actually make the effort to learn it.

When I was still an apprentice, I played rugby for a club in town. I played rugby at school, but never at my fullest potential. The reason for this was because I was always afraid of getting hurt. Strangely enough, I got hurt anyway no matter

Chapter 6   Believe in Yourself

how careful I was trying to be. This was a valuable lesson for me, as I realised that rugby is a dangerous game, it was my choice to play it, and I should give it my all. When I came back to the club after recovering from torn ligaments in my knee, I decided to go out there and play my heart out. And you know what, I played the best rugby I ever played in my life and I moved from the third team to the first team in only two games.

You need to get rid of the fear and delve into the passion and you will achieve great things.

Once you start achieving more smaller goals, it will start to build your confidence level and make you want to try larger goals. Nobody can set your goals for you; you need to do it yourself.

Develop that unmistakable belief that you can achieve anything and you will be able to achieve anything. Take control of your destiny and find that one thing in your life that drives you to your ultimate best.

Remember that in each of us is a God-given gift, a skill, or something that you can do that nobody else had to teach you how to do. There is no one else that can beat you at it and no one else can do it for you. Very often, it might be the thing that scares you the most.

For me, it was public speaking. I used to go into a panicked state and literally start shaking if I had to speak in front of

Chapter 6   Believe in Yourself

people, even though I always admired people that could talk in front of large crowds and make it seem so effortless. It was not because I could not speak or I had nothing to say, it was because I did not believe in myself and I was afraid of what others might think.

I finally got up and started speaking in front of people after I got involved with a network marketing company. At one training event, my good friend and upline encouraged me to do a small part of the training. Just the notion of me getting up in front of all those people to speak scared me, and I did not want to do it at first, but I knew that deep down inside of me I wanted to try it at least once. My friend also gave me a great piece of advice, he said, *"Remember, most of the people sitting there have no idea how it should be done, so they won't know if you make a mistake."* That put me at ease a little bit, even if it was only enough to get me to stand up and go to the front of the room. Then my inner desire had to take over and get me through it.

The great thing about the network marketing company I was involved with at the time was that the people genuinely supported me and wanted me to succeed, and it's like that in most network marketing companies. They encouraged me and helped me through that first time and I really learned a lot from that. I then went to more and more training sessions to learn from other speakers. I started volunteering to do small parts of the training and pretty soon, I had gotten confident enough to try a bigger training event.

Chapter 6   Believe in Yourself

My first big training session was a forty-five-minute training session on how to do retail and find new customers. Having spent many hours at training, I knew exactly what the process was to follow and I almost knew the training off the top my head. I gave my training in front of approximately eighty people. I could literally feel my pants shake on my body because I was so nervous, but as I got into the training, I started to speak with passion, my nervousness subsided, and I started to enjoy what I was doing. Seeing the way the crowd responded to my words, their faces lighting up at what I said, and the laughter when I told a joke, all made me feel like I was truly making a difference in their lives by helping them to understand the concepts of the business in a fun way.

It definitely helped that I was very passionate about the products and the company, and the training went really well. When I finished my training, I actually got a standing ovation! I was so surprised and smiled from ear to ear. I had never before experienced such a feeling of accomplishment ever in my life before then.

Afterward, one of the gentlemen who at that stage had been in the business for more than twelve years, came to me and said that it was one of the best retail trainings he had seen in his entire time with the company. That was probably the biggest compliment I have ever received. And to think, when I was at school I could hardly read out of my book in front of the class.

Chapter 6 Believe in Yourself

The fact is that if I did not try that first small training, then I would have never done the bigger training and a lot of people might have missed out on what I had to teach that day, including me. Believe me, I learned a lot about myself that day that has helped me develop into the person I am today and will continue to help me develop into the person I want to be in the future.

I have come to realise that every single person on this planet has something to offer and a lot to teach. They just lack the self-confidence to do anything about it. This was exactly the same place I was at, at one stage in my life. People are so afraid of what others think of them or what they might say that they are too scared to try. They are scared that they might make a mistake and be laughed at or made fun of.

Let me tell you something that I learned through a lot of self-reflection and lots of effort. You can be whoever you want to be and what other people think of you does not have to define who you are! Les Brown believed that he was a slow learner and mentally retarded due to something that a teacher said. That belief became so real to him that he always doubted himself and his ability to learn until a wise teacher gave him the best advice ever. He said, *"Someone's opinion of you does not have to become your reality."*

So many times, we believe what other people say and make that our reality. This is one of the biggest contributing factors to bad self-esteem. Remember that in God's eyes we are all of equal value! No one person is better than anybody else, and

Chapter 6   Believe in Yourself

you should never let anyone make you believe that you are worthless! You are an amazing creation and an awesome child of God. Start living up to that reputation and become the best version of you that you can be.

Marianne Williamson said, *"Our biggest fear is not that we are inadequate; our biggest fear is that we are powerful beyond measure."* I think many times we are more scared of success than we are of failure. It scares us that we might actually succeed and not be able to handle that success. Or, we are afraid of what or who we will become when we are successful. Remember that for almost all of the self-made millionaires in the world, success and money did not change them, it only made them more of who they were before they were successful. Money is a magnifier. If you are a caring, compassionate person before you are successful, then you will be even more so when you are successful.

The fact is that no matter what it is you want to achieve in life, you first need to believe that it is possible. You first need to believe that you can achieve it. Therefore, it is of utmost importance to stop all the negative self-talk you might be doing, start reinforcing yourself with positive messages, and start believing that you can achieve anything you set your mind to! You are powerful beyond measure.

If you start believing in yourself, you will start to attract other people to you that will also believe in you. You will start to attract positive things to you and you will start seeing things pulling you towards your dreams. This does not mean that

Chapter 6 Believe in Yourself

magic suddenly starts to happen and everything just falls into place. It all happens because when you start changing your self-talk and self-belief, you start to open your eyes to the possibilities out there. You start seeing things that you never saw before, even if it has always been there. If you have an open mind, your eyes will be open to seeing all the possibilities.

Once I started to change my thinking, I started seeing many new opportunities for me to follow my dreams, I met new people, and I was offered opportunities to share my story and speak to others. My business started to expand, and so did my income. I started making more friends and was invited to more and more networking events where I met even more people that opened more opportunities.

Changing the way you see yourself has massive power to change your future. Do not focus on where you are now! Start seeing yourself where you want to be and start acting as if you are already there. If you start acting like a successful person and dress like a successful person, then you will start to feel like a successful person, and in turn, become successful.

Create a vivid picture of yourself at the level you want to be. What will you do? Where will you live? What car will you drive? How will you act?

Then, start acting like you are already there. Pretty soon, you will start to believe that you are already there, and other people will also start to see you at that level.

Chapter 6   Believe in Yourself

Jim Rohn says, *"For things to change you have to change."*

Go now and do some self-reflection. Look at what you want to change about yourself and start making small little changes one at a time. Before long you will be a brand new you, ready to take on whatever the world can throw at you. No matter how tough it may get, never stop believing in yourself.

"We can't become what we need to be by remaining what we are."

Oprah Winfrey

Chapter 6 Believe in Yourself

Chapter 6 Believe in Yourself

Chapter 7

Prepare Yourself

As stated in the previous chapter, believing in yourself is one of the most important parts to achieving your ultimate goals, but self-belief alone will not change anything. You need to take action and put plans in place to help you achieve your goals. You will stay trapped inside your comfort zone forever if you don't learn to take action.

My wife always says, *"Faith without action means nothing,"* meaning that I could believe in myself and have all the best plans, but if I did not take action and start moving in the direction of my goals, then I would stay exactly where I was. I had to start doing something about my situation and stop living on dreams. Remember that a goal without a plan is just a wish, and a plan without action is just a possibility, but if you take action, it can become a reality.

Another important factor to remember is that you cannot take action if you do not have a plan. You do not start a journey if you do not yet know the destination. Once you know the destination, you need to plan your route, otherwise, you will get lost. It is the same in our lives. We need to write

Chapter 7   Prepare Yourself

down our goals so that we have a destination, but then we need to plan our route so that we can reach our goals. Determine what you need to do to achieve your goals and start preparing yourself and developing yourself along the way. You need to be prepared for when an opportunity comes your way.

Whitney M. Young, Jr. says, *"It is better to be prepared for an opportunity and not have one than to have an opportunity and not be prepared."*

Imagine what you would feel like if you get the opportunity of a lifetime and you are not prepared to take advantage of that opportunity, and it slips through your fingers. Other opportunities will come by, but you will never get back the ones you let slip by. Be prepared!

It is truly amazing how many opportunities start to come your way once you make yourself ready to receive them.

Before my first opportunity to speak presented itself, I started to prepare myself. I started listening to audio programmes of motivational speakers. I listened to what they had to say and how they said it. I took notes and started writing down my ideas. I listened to them over and over again and each time I learned something new. I started learning the best practices from the professionals in the business without having ever met them.

There are millions of professionals in the world who we can learn from, people who are more than willing to teach the

Chapter 7   Prepare Yourself

skills they learned through years of struggles and hard work. Many of these great speakers also offer a lot of free content and newsletters to anyone who wants it; all you need to do is look for it.

Start preparing yourself for your future success! Look for people that already achieved what you would like to achieve. Start reading their books if they have any. Start looking on the internet for blogs, forums, books, or websites on the topic that you would like to further your knowledge in. The internet has made it easier than ever for anyone to be able to find exactly what they are looking for.

One of my biggest excuses that I always used was that I disliked reading. I was not the best or fastest reader and because of eyestrain, I used to get headaches when I read. This kept me from reading anything and I wasted a lot of my time in front of the TV, or *"idiot box"* as my wife used to call it. Finally, I discovered audiobooks that really helped me a lot, and it was in one of those audiobooks that I learned one of the most important lessons from Zig Ziglar that completely changed my outlook on reading. Zig said that *"The person who will not read is no better off than the person who cannot read."* To me, this was a very profound statement, and it is absolutely true. It made me realise that if I did not read because of whatever excuse, then I was in no better position than a person who could not read.

I realised that there are millions of people around the world that would love to have the ability to read, but unfortunately,

Chapter 7   Prepare Yourself

they don't. They would do anything to be able to read a storybook to their children at night or study to be able to get a job. And yet, I was in this fortunate position and did not use it.

That was when I decided to start reading as much as I could. I would look for audiobooks where I could and sometimes I would listen to the audiobooks while reading the hard copy. I was never going to let my own excuses keep me from my ultimate success.

I realised that the only one keeping me from being successful was me and that I needed to change myself and educate myself in order to become the person I wanted to be. In essence, I was creating my ultimate state of readiness.

In any defence force around the world, the soldiers practice many hours to prepare for what may happen. Even in countries that are not at war, they are still practicing. They practice until they achieve a level of preparedness where they can respond to any threat in a matter of minutes and then they keep practicing to maintain that level of preparedness or readiness. You cannot prepare once and then think you are ready. You need to keep at it and stay sharp. Do not lose your focus and do not slack your efforts. Keep preparing so that when your opportunity comes, you are ready.

Chapter 7 Prepare Yourself

In the movie **Facing the Giants**, they tell the story of two farmers who desperately needed rain. Both of them prayed for rain, but only one of them went out and prepared his fields to receive it.

This is a beautifully simple example of how many people are asking and praying for their opportunities to come, but they never prepare for them. Then, when the opportunity does come, it is seized by the person who was ready and prepared.

The question is, which one are you going to be? Are you going to be ready for when your opportunity comes, or are you just going to sit around and hope for it to happen?

Remember, good things might come to those who wait, but great things come to those who are prepared!

Another favourite saying of so many people is, *"One day when my ship comes in I will do it."* My parents and siblings used to say this so many times. One day I was just fed up of the constant nagging about their current position and how everything would be better when their ship comes in. I stood up and told them that you can never expect a ship to come in if you never sent one out. Even the Bible says that you cannot expect to reap if you have not sown.

Start preparing your fields to receive the rain! You might only plant one seed, but from that one seed, you can get many fruits! The amazing thing is, if you plant an avocado seed, you get a huge avocado tree that will produce many avocados for many years to come. And to think, you only had to plant one

Chapter 7 Prepare Yourself

seed to receive all those avocados. The same principle works with anything in life. If you prepare now and put in the effort now, it will pay you hundredfold in the future. Also remember that when a tree is small it needs a lot of care and protection against the elements, but as it gets bigger and stronger and it starts to develop strong roots, then it becomes almost completely self-sufficient.

With self-belief it works the same way: first, you need a lot of support and reinforcement, but soon you will be strong and able to keep going through the toughest of times.

Start taking steps in the direction you want to go. You might not get there overnight, but you will get there. You can change your direction right now and end up in a much better place a few months or years from now.

Never think that you can just stay the way you are and things will never change! That is naïve! Remember that the world is constantly evolving and if you don't change with it, you will end up in a place you don't want to be, wondering how you got there.

People always say that you shouldn't try to re-invent the wheel, but you shouldn't throw away the wheel either. Learn from other people and the mistakes they made. Being the youngest of five kids in my family, I had the great blessing of being able to learn from my brother and three sisters. I could see what they did that did not work and learn from it. I applied what I learned to my life and it was most valuable to

Chapter 7   Prepare Yourself

me. I still made my own mistakes, but that is what life is about, getting those challenges and rising above them.

Many people have the same opportunity to learn from other people, but because of their stubbornness, they choose to go their own way and do their own thing, often making the exact same mistakes again. Those mistakes could have been avoided if they only learned from those who went before them!

Get out there and find what drives you and start running toward your dreams. Start preparing yourself to be ready for when your opportunities arrive. Be willing to do whatever it takes for you to conquer your fears and achieve your goals. No dream is too big or too small, so don't let anything or anybody stand in your way.

The third way to prepare yourself and shave years from your learning time is to find people that can help you.

This includes finding yourself a good mentor. Then, spend as much time with them as you can, asking as many questions as possible, to learn everything they have to teach you. Then, find another and another! You cannot have too many mentors. Find someone who already achieved the success you would like to achieve and learn from them. There is always a way to get to where you want to go, you just need to look for it hard enough.

Chapter 7   Prepare Yourself

If you are like me and have a dream to become a pilot, then go to the airports and start talking to the pilots there. Start doing self-study on how to become a pilot. Find flying manuals and start studying the principles of flight. Get a flight simulator and start practicing. Be prepared for your opportunity!

When my opportunity finally came to do my first flight, I was so well prepared that I flew my entire first flight, from take-off to landing, with almost no input from my instructor. I was preparing for years for that moment and when it finally arrived, I was ready. Because of my preparation, I managed to do my first solo flight after just five hours of instruction.

What I did was nothing special, and anybody can do it if they are willing to do the same things I did to reach their goals.

No matter what your dream is, you can achieve it! Just go out and prepare yourself. The more time you spend preparing yourself, the easier it will be to take advantage of the opportunities when they arrive. I suggest reading as many books on your chosen topic as you can find. If you can't find hard copies of books, then sign up for a Kindle account and read online. If you are like me and are better with auditory learning, then sign up for an Audible account. I have listened to much more books than I have read over the years, and struggling to read is not an excuse to not learn from books. Remember that books are an incredibly valuable source of knowledge, but having a mentor that can guide you step by step is priceless, so find yourself a good one.

Chapter 7 Prepare Yourself

Be ready for when your opportunity comes.

Chapter 7 Prepare Yourself

Chapter 8

Creating Opportunities Through Networking

To help you break free from the zone you need to have something to look forward to. That is where opportunities come in. There are so many opportunities out there for you to be able to achieve your goals, but until you are ready, you might miss them.

It is also possible to create your own opportunities.

When I got involved in network marketing, I really started to grasp this concept. The answer was in the name itself, "Networking."

There are so many people involved in network marketing today that completely forget about the networking and they only want to do the marketing. This is such a big mistake because the biggest power of network marketing lies in networking. Some of my best customers and business partners were referred to me by friends, family, or connections I made through networking. Just from me getting involved with a networking group, I increased my

Chapter 8   Creating Opportunities Through Networking

sales and opened other opportunities for me in other ventures as well.

Networking is one of the most powerful methods of building success and creating opportunities.

Remember that once you start networking, you are basically marketing yourself and what you have to offer others. This is not only in your own business capacity, but in also what you can do for their business. Remember that successful networking is a sharing and giving relationship. If you want to do it purely to get more business and you don't give back, then you will quickly loose rapport with the group and this damages your business, your reputation, and also limits, or sometimes even kills, other opportunities.

One of the biggest killers of rapport is dishonesty. So many people think that their dishonesty is so small that others will not realise it, but they do notice it. If you become known as dishonest and you lose credibility, then nobody is going to buy from you or refer other people to you, and I know that a good referral is the best business you can get.

One thing I have always strived for was to be completely honest in all my business dealings and in my personal life. You can't act like this wonderfully honest businessman if you are lying to your wife. Be honest in all aspects of your life! People are not stupid. They see much more than you think they do.

Chapter 8   Creating Opportunities Through Networking

It is definitely worth reading more about how to network successfully. As I said, it is a very powerful business tool that will do wonders for you and your business if done correctly.

When I was still a young man, I was still very shy and had a terribly low self-esteem. I never spoke to somebody that I did not know or was not introduced to unless they initiated the conversation. This was such a self-limiting thing for me to do, but I did not realise it at the time. I was so bad that one of my close friend's wife told me that when she first met me she thought I was incredibly rude. Luckily, she got to know me better and saw that I was a really nice guy. However, that really got me thinking, and it made me wonder, if that was the image I was putting out to the world, then what must people think of me? I was giving people the wrong image about myself without even knowing it and this was hurting me socially and financially in my business.

Think carefully about the image you are projecting to people who don't know you. Do they see you as an open, friendly person, or as a closed and grumpy person? Remember that most people create an opinion about you within a couple of seconds, and if you are putting an image out there that is not very friendly, then they will avoid you. I was causing people not to like me by not showing them the real me.

I can tell you now that I have changed dramatically and people who knew me then and see me now can't believe that I am the same person. In a sense, I am still the same person, but personality wise I am totally different. I am kinder, more

Chapter 8   Creating Opportunities Through Networking

open, and I smile more. I am much more willing to start a conversation with a stranger, yet I still have room for improvement. The more I meet new people and make new friends, the easier it gets and the more confident I become, and the more confident I become, the easier it gets. It is as if I have created perpetual motion that continues to pick up speed and become more powerful as time goes by.

Now I must admit that I have also had to deal with a couple of weird, stuck up, or just downright rude people, and many times the experience wanted to force me back into my shell to just hide away from the world, but then I would tell myself to keep going. As they say, "If you fall off the horse, get back on immediately." I just turned around, found someone else, and started again, and oftentimes the very next person is the most pleasant and friendly person that just restores your faith in mankind. I realised that I was exactly like the other rude people, not intentionally, but that is how I came across to the people who met me. I was acting like a jerk through my inaction and unwillingness to open up to others due to my own self-doubt.

Luckily, I realised my mistake and immediately started to make some changes. Now whenever I walk past anyone, I smile, look them straight in the eye, and say, "hello." You will not believe what a response this creates from the people. Some immediately smile and greet you back, others just look at you like you are crazy, and others look away and act as if they did not hear you. This is due to their bad self-image and

Chapter 8   Creating Opportunities Through Networking

it has nothing to do with you personally, so don't take it personally. Just keep smiling and hold your head up high.

While I was working at a very large stainless steel manufacturing plant, I started employing my new tactics on the people around me. There was one individual that never returned my greeting; he would just look away and walk past. At first, I thought to myself that I was not going to greet him again, but I thought about words commonly attributed to Gandhi, *"Be the change you want to see in the world."* I decided to just keep on greeting him every time I saw him no matter what. It took me about two months of unreturned greetings before he started to return my greetings. At first, it was just a nod, then it turned into a mumble, and just before I left the company, he would actually stop by my office just to say hello. Never give up on anybody; you don't know what their situation is or what they are going through. Your little bit of kindness might be the only kindness they get and they might not know how to handle it yet.

This has proven to be very valuable to me in my network marketing business and in my personal life. I have many more friends from all walks of life. My business has picked up, I have many new customers, and my customers are referring new customers. I have also received various other great business opportunities, mostly through the people I met that I treated kindly and with respect.

Make sure that the image you put out for the world to see is a good one. First impressions might not be absolute, but they

Chapter 8   Creating Opportunities Through Networking

are very powerful, and it will take you a long time to correct a bad first impression.

Always respond to invitations to networking opportunities. The more the people see you at networking events, the more comfortable they will become with you, and this, in turn, will start to create more opportunities. Use every single opportunity you can to meet new contacts. Allow yourself the opportunity to become comfortable with other people. As they become more comfortable with you, they will start inviting you to more and more events.

You also need to be at the right place at the right time for when your opportunity might come knocking. This can happen anywhere at any time, so you need to be available and prepared for it. It will never happen if you always choose to stay at home to watch TV and you don't take the chances you have to network. You need to get in amongst people to find opportunity because they can come in all shapes and sizes and sometimes when you least expect it.

You can see that by creating a more likeable person in yourself, you will automatically attract other people to you. People that like you are far more likely to do business with you.

Be honest, friendly, and trustworthy in everything you do, and this will cause people to always keep you in high esteem. If opportunities arise where honest and trustworthy people are wanted, then your name will definitely be mentioned. This

Chapter 8   Creating Opportunities Through Networking

does not mean you will get every opportunity, but the more your name is mentioned, the higher your chances of success.

In truth, many of my first opportunities came out of friendships that I created from people that I met while networking. The people knew the product and the company, but until they truly knew and trusted me, they were not completely willing to freely do business with me. Once the trust was established, the opportunities and new business clients started flowing in.

Very few opportunities just happen out of the blue or just fall into your lap. Most of the opportunities you get will come from the people you know and the contacts you have made. Make use of them wisely and handle them properly and you will get much more. Opportunities are endless if you know where to look. So in essence, opportunities do not just happen, nor do they just lie around for anyone to see. You need to go look for them, chase after them, and most importantly, become worthy of them.

Many people believe that the Bible says that God will not give you more than you can handle. This is not true. The fact is that God does allow more challenges than we can handle. I don't believe that God gives us those struggles, the enemy does that. God helps us through it. We need Him to overcome those things that we are powerless to overcome on our own. What I believe to be true is that God will never let us go through the difficult times alone and that He will always

Chapter 8   Creating Opportunities Through Networking

instruct us and comfort us through the process. Many believe that this is only referring to hardships, but I believe it is with everything in life. If you trust God to teach you how to handle your money wisely, then you will be blessed with more. If you are faithful and use the abilities God has given you, then He will give you more. And if you trust God to guide you in how to identify and seize opportunities, then you will see opportunities everywhere. Don't wait until you get more to do better, first learn to do better and then you will get more.

The ability is in all of us to rise above our trials and tribulations and make the best of our lives, but the choice is ours. Nobody can make the choice for you. It is something you have to do on your own, but you can do it!

Start with what you have right now, however small it may be, and then progress from there. Always do more than what you get paid to do. This will make you the most valuable employee in your company and soon they will start paying you more to keep you. If they don't, then another company will come to hear about you and offer you more. The point is that you first need to become more valuable before the opportunity will come.

"Work harder on yourself than you do on your job."

Jim Rohn

Chapter 8   Creating Opportunities Through Networking

This is one of the most powerful statements I have learned and it has truly changed my life. Only when I increased the value I added to others, did my situation and income start to change. If you add more value, you earn more money.

I needed to work through my self-doubt and self-limiting beliefs, and I needed to start believing that I was valuable and that I was capable of doing whatever I set my mind to. Once I started to believe that, my life started to change. Not only my finances changed, but everything in my life changed, too. I am now constantly doing more than is expected of me, not only by others but by myself, too. Sometimes we expect too little from ourselves. We should push our limits to reach new heights. It is widely believed that most humans use less than ten percent of their brains at any one time and that we have so much more untapped potential. I believe that this is the same with our physical abilities. We are capable of far more than we give ourselves credit for, but we have become complacent and afraid to live up to our true potential. Remember, you can teach yourself new skills every day to improve your abilities.

The more willing we are to get out of our comfort zone and into new environments, the more opportunities will come our way. Go look for them at the right places. You will never go to a clothing store to find hardware, and you will never go to a hardware store to buy a computer or cell phone. You go to the correct shop to find the correct items. Likewise, you should go to the correct places to meet the people that will

Chapter 8   Creating Opportunities Through Networking

advance you in a certain area. Some great advice from George Clason's book **The Richest Man in Babylon,** is that we should never take the advice of a brick maker about jewels, but instead go to the jewel merchant.

This is very wise advice, yet so many of us take the advice of our friends, family, or anyone willing to give advice. We never consider the fact that they themselves have absolutely no knowledge about the subject.

Listen to wise men who are experienced in the field you want to go in, and spend time with them. Learn all you can, and in time, your opportunities will come.

The fourth way to finding your potential is to never stop looking for opportunities.

Create your network by finding the right people willing to teach you and help you to reach the top.

Chapter 8   Creating Opportunities Through Networking

Chapter 8 Creating Opportunities Through Networking

Chapter 9

Teach

"If your actions inspire others to dream more, learn more, do more, and become more, then you are a leader."

John Quincy Adams

I love this quote from John Quincy Adams. It simply encompasses the true meaning of helping others. If we can make others see their own potential inside them and help them want to achieve more, then that brings so much joy and purpose to our lives. There is nothing more satisfying than seeing someone who had nothing become successful by applying the skills that you have taught them. Become comfortable teaching others and your journey from your comfort zone will be a pleasant one.

The first thing I did after I became involved with the network marketing business was to find people that needed my help, people that wanted to change their lives, but did not know how. I found a couple of people with so much potential, but

Chapter 9   Teach

they just weren't ready to change themselves and to create those opportunities to be successful. Then I met some people with very little talent, but so much passion and heart and willingness to learn that nothing could stand in their way. These people were like sponges sucking up everything I had to teach them. They listened to me intently when I spoke and little by little, their confidence grew and with that confidence, so did their businesses.

With many of these people, I became close friends. That is the beauty of business and motivation. You attract like-minded people to yourself and in turn, increase your circle of friends. And one of the greatest things for me was the wonderful things I, myself, learned from every single one of those people. You see when you teach someone, it is very important to not only be a teacher but to also be a student. Like I said before, everybody has something to teach, but we must be ready to learn. Don't think just because somebody else got into the business after you did, or someone is younger than you, or someone is not as wealthy as you, that they do not have something to teach you. I have learnt some of my biggest life lessons from people that were my subordinates.

> *"God calls us not to be successful, but to be significant.*
> *When we focus on significance,*
> *success is often part of the package."*
>
> *Tom Ziglar*

Chapter 9   Teach

One gentleman that I would like to mention is one of the people that I met through my network marketing business. He has now become one of my close friends. He is an African gentleman, and even though when you talk to him he will tell you that I have changed his life, in turn, he has changed mine.

He is just one of those people that continue going no matter what. Whenever something came across his path and just pulled the rug out from under him, he would just get up, dust himself off, ask me what he must do, and then he would do it. Sometimes some of the things that happened to him would have completely floored me, but not him. Everyone who met him would tell you that they have never met someone with as much energy and perseverance like he has. He just never stops and he always has a smile on his face.

There were days when I felt down and he would come to me for advice, but after our talk, I would also feel better.

What I have learned through the whole experience is that when you uplift others, you cannot help but to uplift yourself in the process. Positivity is contagious, and when you get amongst other positive people, you cannot help but to become positive yourself.

Les Brown says that if you are the smartest person in your group of friends, then you should make new friends. If you are the most positive person in your group, then you need to find a group with more positive people than you in it. The thing is, it is very difficult to be the only positive person in a

Chapter 9   Teach

group because just as they can feed off your positive energy, they also drain your positive energy with their negativity. And if you do not have another positive person that motivates you, then you will become just as negative as they are.

One of my friends told me a story that I think just fits into this scenario perfectly. He told me that if you were to hit a tuning fork of a certain note, and you bring that tuning fork into the vicinity of another tuning fork of that same note, then the new tuning fork would start to resonate with the first tuning fork without even touching it. Not only that, but the two tuning forks feed off each other's vibrations, and the sound and vibrations can continue for quite some time.

This, to me, was absolutely incredible to hear and I immediately realised that exactly the same thing happens with human beings. When we get into the vicinity of someone with the same mindset as we have, then we immediately start to be attracted to that person. We start to vibrate and resonate just like the tuning forks do, and we feed off each other's energy. That's one of the reasons why you have to find people that share your passion. You have to find people that will uplift you, and you have to find people that need upliftment from you.

While I was involved with our local BNI chapter, I met an incredible lady that was involved with a charitable company focusing on feeding children. This company goes around all over South Africa and feeds homeless and orphaned children. This woman has so much passion for what she does and so

Chapter 9   Teach

much love for the kids that it is just contagious to be around her.

There are so many opportunities out there in the world where you can apply your skills and your talents to make a difference. But, the biggest thing that we all have to give in abundance, is love. Having been involved in a local charity, I have seen firsthand just how hungry these kids are for a little bit of interaction, love, and affection. Never miss an opportunity to show love. For some people, that might be the first glimpse of love that they have ever experienced.

"And we urge you, brothers and sisters, warn those who are idle and disruptive, encourage the disheartened, help the weak, be patient with everyone."

1 Thessalonians 5:14 (NIV)

I am one of those people that would give the last bit of money I had left in my wallet to someone that needs it, but what I needed to learn was that you cannot give at the expense of yourself. You can only give what you have to give. I once heard someone say that you can help many people around the world, but you have to get rich first. He then went on to explain that when you are poor, what you can give is limited to your own physical ability and presence, but when you are rich, you can help many people all over the world. You see, money gives you the reach to go all over the world and touch people in many nations. This does not mean you shouldn't give until you get rich. That is not walking in love. For me,

Chapter 9   Teach

what is more powerful about this statement is that we all have a responsibility to be successful and do our best to become wealthy in order for us to be able to make a bigger difference in the world and help more people.

"Life is an echo. What you send out, comes back. What you sow, you reap. What you give, you get. What you see in others, exists in you. Remember. Life is an echo. It always gets back to you. So give goodness."

T. Harv Eker

The Bible says that "what you sow, you shall reap," but I believe that it goes much deeper than that. Think about any seed. When you plant a single seed, you get a plant that carries many fruits, and inside these fruits are many more seeds than the one that you have planted. If you were to take those seeds and plant them again, your harvest will continue to grow. That way, what we sow multiplies infinitely. Don't you think that's a nice way to realise that if you make a small difference in someone's life, that one act of kindness creates a ripple effect that can go all around the world?

It is said that we are all spiritual beings inside a physical body. And I believe that when we show random acts of kindness to other people that our spiritual beings interconnect and we create a lasting bond with that person.

Chapter 9   Teach

"No one has ever become poor by giving."

Anne Frank

I have to admit that I really love helping people, and I will go out of my way to make them happy. Sadness is inevitable, but no one needs to go through the sadness alone. We can all be there for someone in need, even if it is just by giving them a hug. I don't think we will ever realise the exact power that lies within a hug from someone that truly cares. Go out there and share your love. The more you give, the more you get. That is the way the universe works.

There are so many places that you can find stories about life changing events and about people who have made a huge difference in the world through random acts of kindness.

One of the stories that really touched me is the story about a lady in America. Having had a very rough childhood being in jail at 12, a mother at 14, and homeless at the age of 16, she definitely had her fair share of challenges. At the time of writing this book, she is 79 years old and the mother of nine and can truly empathize with many of the people that she helps. You see, as a teenager in Detroit, she had her life turned around by a caring family who helped her gain and master the tools to succeed and grow.

This lady has such a big heart and has made such a big difference in her community.

Chapter 9 Teach

"The purpose of life is not to be happy. It is to be useful, to be honorable, to be compassionate, to have it make some difference that you have lived and lived well."

Ralph Waldo Emerson

There are so many stories that can be told about ordinary people in ordinary communities that have made extraordinary differences. There's an old proverb that says that God does not choose perfect people, but that he chooses willing people. If you are willing to help others, it does not matter whether you are qualified or not. It only matters if you care enough to help others. That is the only qualifying criteria you need, a willing heart and a love for people.

Zig Ziglar told a story about an old man and his grandson walking along the beach. All along the beach, there were a whole bunch of sand dollars that had been washed out by the ocean. As they walked along, every now and then the grandfather would pick up a sand dollar and toss it back into the ocean. After a while, the little boy asked his grandfather why he was throwing the sand dollars back, and that since there were so many, he would never be able to throw all of them back. The grandfather picked up another sand dollar, looked at the boy and said, "That may be true, but for this one, it makes all the difference in the world."

So many times, you tell yourself that you are only one person, and what difference could you possibly make? This story is

Chapter 9   Teach

evidence that you might not change the whole world at once, but for the one or two people that you can help, it makes all the difference in the world. Don't let your current small-mindedness hold you back from making a huge difference in someone else's life.

Always remember that whenever you help someone else, you cannot help but to help yourself. When you uplift someone else, then it is impossible not to also uplift yourself.

Beyond any doubt, the greatest gift we have to give to others is our own personal knowledge and experience. Every one of us should become teachers.

In one of his life changing seminars, Jim Rohn said that the great thing about teaching is that if you tell ten people something, they hear it only once, but you hear it ten times. This means that while you are teaching others, you are educating yourself. Every time you share, you grow a little bit more. I truly believe that you can only begin to be your best once you start to help others and teach them how to become better skilled in whatever area you can help them.

"The best antidote I know for worry is work. The best cure for weariness is the challenge of helping someone who is even more tired. One of the great ironies of life is this: He or she who serves almost always benefits more than he or she who is served."

Gordon B. Hinckley

Chapter 9   Teach

For many years, I was under the impression that I didn't have much to teach, until one day I sat down and read through my own resume. I realised that I had so much experience that I could share with others. When was the last time that you read through your resume like a recruiter would do, or a potential employer? Look at your skills and abilities. It is time to realise that you have a lot to teach, and a lot to give.

I believe that giving is one of the greatest tools we can use to develop ourselves into great people and great leaders. Not only should we give, but we should freely give. I like to represent it in a form of a glass that is filled with water. If you do not start to pour some out into other glasses, then there will never be room in the glass for fresh water. In the same way, if we do not pour out our knowledge and skills to others, there will never be space in us for more skills and knowledge. The difference for us, though, is that we have the ability to expand and learn more and more, whereas the glass is limited by its size. We have the amazing ability to become whatever we want to be; we can reshape ourselves and become like new.

No matter what your past was like, that does not mean you have nothing to teach. Never let your past dictate your future! You can decide today that you want to do something else, or become someone else and you can start your journey right now.

Embrace your past and use the lessons that you have learned. Remember that a mistake is only a mistake if you do not learn

Chapter 9   Teach

from it. Learn from a mistake and turn it into a lesson. Life was never meant to be perfect, and neither was any human being meant to be. Life should be challenging in order to make us grow, just like a muscle needs to be pushed beyond its limits in order to grow bigger and stronger.

One thing that is also very important is to not judge any person or think that they are below you. When you judge others, you close your mind to what they may have to teach you. When you learn these new skills, it adds to the things that you can teach others. Some of the most valuable lessons I learned were from people much younger than me. Children sometimes have the most amazing insight and imagination, and we should never think less of their ideas just because of their young age. Always be willing to learn from anyone!

Live your life with an open mind, and don't be ignorant. Just because something might not make sense to you right now, does not mean that it is impossible. By learning new things that may seem strange to you, you expand your mind and improve your learning ability. The more you learn, the more you have to teach.

I have seen many older gentlemen in my career that were so set in their ways that they never took any advice from anyone. One of these cases was when I was working at a large chrome smelter factory. One of our large extraction fans was experiencing extreme wear due to large dust particles being sucked through the fan daily. The engineers planned to install massive cyclones at the suction end of the fans to remove

Chapter 9   Teach

most of the larger dust particles. During the manufacturing process, I enquired as to why there were no wear linings inside the cyclones to prevent it from excess wear. I had a lot of experience with cyclones and knew that a wear lining was essential. The engineer told me that there was no way that the cyclone would get damaged by the dust and passed over my suggestion to install a ceramic wear lining. Less than a month after commissioning the cyclones, the first holes started to appear, and in less than six months, the entire cyclone needed to be replaced. If the engineer just listened to me, someone who was just an artisan at that time, it would have extended the life of the cyclone by at least another two years, or even more if the lining was installed properly and maintained properly.

Always be willing to learn, and always be willing to teach.

There is an old Buddhist proverb that says, *"When the student is ready the master appears."* This means that until you are ready to learn the lesson, there will be no teacher. It is not really that there is no teacher, but because of your limited thinking or unwillingness to learn, you cannot see the teacher, but once you are willing to learn, then you will find your teacher, and many times, it is someone that has been there all along. Remember that once you are willing to learn, anybody can be your teacher, because everyone has something to teach.

The best way to ensure that you ingrain what you have learned into your mind is by teaching it to others. I like to put a new twist on "when the student is ready, the master will come,"

Chapter 9 Teach

and say that when the master is ready, the students will come. This means that when you are ready to teach, then people will show up to hear what you have to teach them. There are many people around the world that can learn from you, but first you need to realise that you have something to teach. Every single one of us has something to teach, we just need to find out what that something is. I also believe that when the student is truly ready to learn, then they realise that everyone can be a master. Even people that have been around you all along can teach you things, not because they became smarter, but because you became more receptive to their knowledge.

Some of my friends now call me their motivator and say that they always feel better after they have spoken to me. It brings so much joy into my heart to hear someone say that having me in their life makes it better. There are many people who are suffering and going through difficult situations, looking for someone to talk to. Why don't you be that person for them? I think one of the biggest gifts you can give to someone is an ear to listen. Never judge, but listen. Don't try to solve all their problems because that's impossible. We cannot take away all the problems in the world, but we can support those going through their troubles and make sure that they realise that they are not alone.

I think in the same way, it can be said that if you are ready to teach, then look for a worthy student. Do not waste your time to try to force somebody to learn from you; they will come when they are ready. Just give them support and guidance and in time they will come to you for advice.

Chapter 9   Teach

I always wanted to be a good leader, and I believed that I had good leadership abilities, but I learned a valuable lesson from Chris Widener. Chris says that you cannot one day decide to be a great leader. You can only become a person that other people would want to follow. The choice lies with them, and if they don't trust you or look up to you, then they will not follow you.

So many people only want to teach a little bit about what they know because they are afraid that the other person will outshine them. Remember earlier when I said that you shouldn't just give, but you should give freely? Keeping your best skills for yourself is a selfish thing and it is limiting you, not the other person. Remember that if you give freely of all you know, then that person will become an inspiration to someone else, and you will have passed on something that has the ability to change the world.

This is a profound statement, and I believe that it is the concept of paying it forward. The little things you do can have the most profound impact on other people's lives. Remember that your words of encouragement that you speak to someone may also have a profound impact on their lives.

In his seminar, Jim Rohn also said that it is one of the greatest honours to show up in someone else's testimonial. You become immortalised in a sense as long as you pass on your knowledge to others. You live on in them and help them shape the lives of others. Do not let all your knowledge go to

Chapter 9   Teach

the grave with you; share it and let it change the lives of millions of others.

We can never know the full effect that our teachings have on the world, and because of that, we must be careful of what we teach the world. Nowhere is this more evident than in what people teach their children. Children do not do what you tell them to do, they do what you do; they emulate you. You cannot tell them to act and talk a certain way if you are not an example. Unfortunately, today we can see it so many times in South Africa where our leaders say one thing and do another. Traffic police are driving around without safety belts, they talk on their cell phones while driving, and they are speeding. These are the people that are supposed to enforce the law, yet they are breaking it themselves.

In James 3:1 it is written *"Not many of you should become teachers, my fellow believers, because you know that we who teach will be judged more strictly."* (NIV) As a leader, you are doubly accountable for what you do. Lead by example, and don't go out with the mentality that so many South Africans and other people around the world are doing. That is the *"if you can't beat them join them"* mentality. I believe that if more people do the right thing, regardless of what other people are doing, then the world will be a much better place. We as leaders should go out and show the world how it should be done. Now don't fool yourself by saying you are not a leader so it doesn't apply to you! We are all leaders, no matter how small our role might be. Somewhere, there is somebody that is looking up to you,

Chapter 9   Teach

so live up to your responsibility and be a great leader.

Let us all go out and teach the world how to care and love again.

Chapter 9   Teach

Chapter 9 Teach

Chapter 10

Never Stop Learning

According to scientificamerican.com, the human mind is capable of storing so much information that it is estimated it can store as much 2.5 petabytes or 2.5 million gigabytes. However, the true answer to that might never be known, but the fact is that the human brain is an exceptional piece of machinery (if we can call it that). Even from before you are born, your brain starts to process information from your basic bodily functions to being able to hear and recognize your mother's voice. The other day I saw a video clip about a four-year-old girl that is able to speak seven languages fluently. Most adults in the world have hardly mastered one, especially if you look at the standards of school education these days. Why not take up the challenge to continue learning in your journey out of your comfort zone?

No matter how impressive the feat of this four-year-old girl is, the truth is that we are all capable of doing the same thing and so much more. As soon as you start to make a conscious decision to learn something new and you apply your mind power, then you will be able to learn just about anything.

Chapter 10 Never Stop Learning

I see this truth more and more every day with my four-year-old foster son. Since even before he was placed with us two years ago, I made a conscious choice that whenever he asked me anything and I knew the answer, I would tell him the truth. He has learned so quickly and at his young age, has a better understanding of how many things on earth function than I think most teenagers know. I don't make the mistake of thinking he is too small to understand because he is exceptionally smart, and the more I teach him and answer his questions, the smarter he gets.

Our lives are constantly evolving, and especially with the rapid growth of technology today, we cannot afford to sit around. We need to learn and grow to be able to evolve with it.

I have read many stories of people that decided to try something new after retiring, and it became their most significant part of their lives. There was a gentleman in South Africa that worked his entire life as a teacher until the day he retired. Then, he decided that he wanted to become a lawyer, so he studied and got his qualifications as a lawyer and he actively practiced law until his death in his late eighties.

You are never too old, or too young, to learn new things. Remember that your brain, in some aspects, functions like a muscle, and the more you use it, the stronger it gets. That is why there are so many people in their nineties that can still vividly share stories from their childhood and even recall

Chapter 10   Never Stop Learning

names and dates. Don't allow your brain to become stagnant. Remember that stagnant water cannot sustain life for long. There needs to be movement, an inflow of water or air that keeps the oxygen in the water and allows it to sustain life. Like this water, your brain and your knowledge constantly need to keep flowing and moving. Keep adding to it and sharing from it.

One of the worst things I constantly hear is the phrase, "I knew that." The people who say that, always act as if they know everything. This closes their minds to any new information and the possibility of growth. I always grab every opportunity to learn something new. Even if I may have heard it many times before, there might just be a new twist on things, or I might just learn something I didn't hear before. You see, even though you may have heard the same message before, you grow as an individual and because of this, every time you hear it you may learn something new.

Become hungry for knowledge and you will find it everywhere. Read books, listen to audiobooks, watch seminars online. You can even learn a new career, no matter what your age. Start scouring the internet for free education. There are various websites called MOOC's (Massive Open Online Courses) where you can learn various skills almost to the point of a college degree. Even though these might not actually be a formal qualification, the knowledge you gain will certainly help you throughout your life and career. It might even help you gain access to that new elusive career you

Chapter 10 Never Stop Learning

wanted to pursue, but didn't know how to. Bruce Lee once said that the usefulness of the cup is in its emptiness. If a cup is full, then you cannot add anything to it, but when it is empty, there is always room for something in it. Let your mind be like a sponge, always soaking up information. Do not be fooled into thinking you already know everything you need to know for where you are right now in your life or career, but what if that were to change tomorrow? What if someone designs a piece of technology or machine that can replace you tomorrow? How will you handle it then? Start learning new things today, to ensure that you won't become obsolete tomorrow.

"The capacity to learn is a gift, the ability to learn is a skill, the willingness to learn is a choice."

Brian Herbert

Make a choice today to always keep learning. Even though you might not need those skills today, you never know when you might be able to teach those same skills to someone else to make their lives better.

Think of it this way: imagine you had a friend who was blind, did not know how to read braille, and you couldn't read either. If you took the time and made the effort to learn how to read, you would have the ability to read to your friend.

Chapter 10   Never Stop Learning

They, in turn, will hear, learn, and experience many things that they would never have been able to do without you.

All it takes is someone with the willingness to change. You can literally change your future today by deciding to learn a new skill.

Never think that the school education you received is good enough. The fact is that most of the schooling systems today were designed to create workers and not thought pioneers. Free-thinking is not encouraged and if your answer does not match the book answer, then you are deemed to be wrong. Don't just trust someone else's opinion about something. Research it and find your own answers. Don't let other people tell you what to think. Learn to think for yourself as this fuels your creativity.

"Education is what remains after one has forgotten what one has learned in school."

Albert Einstein

Don't think that it will be easy, because it won't. If it were easy, then everyone would do it. The fact is that there are many people that don't really want to change. They complain about their lives, but they are not willing to change it, to learn new things, or to become better. They are content just staying where they are while making everyone around them

Chapter 10   Never Stop Learning

miserable. People like that will always find a way of trying to dissuade you from following your dreams and striving to become better. The reason for this is that when you actually succeed, it makes them feel even worse about themselves. Don't let that stop you.

The fifth way to reaching your potential is to never quit.

You need to become the smartest person you know. Then, use the other skills you learned earlier in this book, find someone smarter, and start the process again, learning as much as you can from them.

The entire learning process is a journey of self-discovery. You find out more about yourself and what you are capable of as you learn more and more.

When I was an apprentice, they taught me all there was to know about how to become a qualified boilermaker artisan. I am a very fast learner and always strive to do my best, so I quickly mastered the basic skills of being a boilermaker. I can tell you, however, that it is only when you are qualified as an artisan and start working by yourself that you truly learn the skills to do your job properly. You truly learn only when you have to solve the problems and figure out what to do on your own. If I came out of my apprenticeship thinking I knew everything and that nobody could teach me anything, then I can tell you that I would have failed quickly and miserably.

Chapter 10   Never Stop Learning

Instead, I stayed humble and kept asking questions from other artisans and pretty soon, I became very good at my job. I also loved helping others with their jobs. Even if it had nothing to do with my trade, I loved helping because I was constantly learning.

If you are an artisan or you have a specific role in a company, then I am pretty sure that you would one day want to move up in the company and become a supervisor or manager. The best way to do that is to understand what other people are doing in the company. Not only will it give you a better understanding of how the company works and what exactly it is that people do, it will also help you earn tremendous respect from those individuals in the company that you might want to lead someday. Believe me, it is much easier to be a good supervisor and leader if the people respect you.

There is a saying that a good leader is someone who can get people to do exactly what he or she wants them to do, not because they are forced to, but because they want to. When people respect you and trust you, they will do what you ask of them, and sometimes you won't even have to ask.

Show people that you value them by showing interest in what they do. By doing this, not only do you learn, but you also make that person feel good about themselves. All people love to feel valued.

Be the kind of person that always strives to know more, and always be willing to share your knowledge.

Chapter 10   Never Stop Learning

Andrew Carnegie had a goal to spend the first half of his life to make all his money and to spend the second part of his life giving it all away. Be the person that spends all your life learning new things and gaining knowledge, and spending the same amount of time giving it all away. Don't keep all your knowledge to yourself. Share it, and make the world a better place.

Chapter 10 Never Stop Learning

Chapter 10   Never Stop Learning

Chapter 11

Always Strive for More

To truly be able to say that you have broken free from your comfort zone, you need to constantly be reinventing yourself. You see, as you progress and reach a new level in your life, it is very tempting to fall back into the same habit of remaining in your comfort zone. The fact is that you always need to grow, learn, get better, create new goals, and follow new dreams. This might sound daunting to you, but the fact is that once you start to experience the excitement of starting something new and reaching your goals, then it becomes easier and very satisfying.

Right now, it might be difficult for you to imagine that you might ever achieve something great, especially if you are in the same place where I used to be. Remember that you are destined for greatness. The only one that can make you stay where and who you are right now is you. And the only one that can change where you are and who you are, is you.

Remember that life is not easy. It was never meant to be easy. Life is meant to be meaningful and satisfying. You were not born to grow up, get a job, work until you retire, and then

Chapter 11   Always Strive for More

struggle to survive until you die. You need to enjoy your life, and the only way to do that is by doing something meaningful with it. This does not mean you need to be the next Mother Teresa. Just don't keep what you have to offer to yourself. Rise up and be the person you always dreamed you could be.

Now, throughout this book we have discussed various things that you can do to make your way out of your comfort zone. It will not happen overnight and it is a lifelong journey because as you grow, your comfort zone grows with you. We will briefly discuss the five ways that you need to focus on if you truly want to see lasting results.

Number one: Always stay positive.

Throughout your life, there will always be things that will challenge you, that will hurt you, and that will change you. For me, it was a devastating car accident. For you, it might be a divorce, dealing with a disability, losing a loved one, fighting a deadly disease, or trying to find your place in a world full of mean people that constantly bully and belittle you.

I might not know what you are going through right now, but I do know that the principles in this book will help you overcome any diversity you might be facing in your life. I constantly remind myself of Job in the Bible. Like Job, we need to trust God and have faith. He is in control, and even though we may not know why we are going through the things we are going through, He sees the bigger picture and He can make every situation turn out good in the end.

Chapter 11 Always Strive for More

Remember that life is full of seasons. You might be going through a very tough winter right now, but the fact is, spring will come, and pretty soon you will experience a marvellous summer again. Life can be beautiful if you choose to always see the best in the world.

I am constantly reminded of the story about twin brothers that were raised by an alcoholic father who used to beat them all the time. Those two boys grew up in exactly the same circumstances, but one turned out just like their father, and the other turned out highly successful and was a loving father. When they were asked why they ended up where they did, they both had a very similar answer. The one brother said, "I grew up with an alcoholic father that constantly beat me. That was my example, how could I turn out any different?" The other said, "I grew up with an alcoholic father that constantly beat me, that was my example, and I made the choice that I never wanted to be like him."

You see, their situation was the same, their answers were almost identical, but their outlooks were worlds apart.

Just like these two brothers, you have a choice. Which one are you going to be?

"Every person has free choice. Free to obey or disobey the Natural Laws. Your choice determines the consequences. Nobody ever did, or ever will, escape the consequences of his choices."

Alfred A. Montapert

Number two: Learn from your experiences.

The second key ties in with the first one. No matter what you are going through, whether it is good or bad, there are many lessons that you can learn. Every situation brings with it valuable life lessons that if you choose to, can teach you remarkable things that will serve you well in your future. You will also be able to help others who might be going through the same thing. Your experience and words of comfort and guidance for someone else might literally be the difference between life and death. There is a vast number of stories from across the world about people that were ready to give up and commit suicide when someone stepped in and helped them through it. Your message, your story, might save somebody's life.

With every difficulty comes opportunity. Many times, when you are at your lowest point in life, it is easier to make major life changes. Why? Because you have nothing left to lose. You can completely redesign your life, and choose to pursue a new goal. You are not a tree. You can move!

So often we hang on so tight to the little bit that we have that we don't see the massive potential all around us. Don't get stuck in the endless pit of self-pity. Learn from your mistakes and your situations and see how you can use them as a stepping stone to success.

Chapter 11   Always Strive for More

"Character cannot be developed in ease and quiet. Only through experience of trial and suffering can the soul be strengthened, ambition inspired, and success achieved."

Helen Keller

Number three: Find people that can help you.

Human beings were not meant to be alone. That is why God created Eve, so Adam could have a wife to share in his experiences with. Don't try to go through your challenges alone.

I have read many accounts of people that lost their minds while being in isolation. Why do you think it was used as a means of mental torture during so many wars? It is easy to lose sight of what is important in your life, or even your will to live if you try to go through challenges alone.

Find someone that can support you through the tough times. Join a support group. When you lose your job, go to a networking event and meet new people. Someone there might be able to help you find new opportunities. Don't go to a bar and sit with the other people that just lost something. The key is to do things differently than other people. When you get knocked down, jump up and immediately look for the next opportunity.

Chapter 11 Always Strive for More

You greatly increase your chances of success by keeping company with a group of people or individuals that can support you and lift you up when you are down.

No one person ever changed the world on their own. It is impossible. You need a support structure. The one man that made the biggest difference in the world was Jesus, and even He had apostles. He needed them to continue His message and work after He was no longer here.

Find yourself a mentor. Someone who will tell you the truth and be straight with you. Remember, your mentor is not a buddy. They need to be someone that can get you moving, and keep you moving. It needs to be someone that won't let you procrastinate and stay in your comfort zone. If you want to move forward, find the right mentor. If you are not sure if someone is the right mentor for you, tell them exactly what you expect from them. If they are not willing to do what you expect, then find someone who will.

"The delicate balance of mentoring someone is not creating them in your own image, but giving them the opportunity to create themselves."

Steven Spielberg

Chapter 11   Always Strive for More

Number four: Always look for opportunities.

Opportunities are endless, and as the world changes, there are more and more opportunities. Just imagines going out into the world in the 1960s telling people that you are going to create an app. They would have thought you were crazy. But today, there are thousands of apps on the market, and new ones are constantly being created.

As I have written earlier in this book, you need to constantly prepare yourself. The skills you may need for your opportunity may not even exist yet, just like in the example of the app, but as the world changes, you need to keep changing with it. If you do that, you can be ready for when your opportunity knocks.

Don't be the person that receives the opportunity of a lifetime, only to lose it to someone else because you weren't ready to seize it.

Remember also that opportunities come in many shapes and sizes. I once heard a story about a man that was caught in a flood. As he was sitting on the roof of his house, he prayed sincerely that God would save him. As the water kept rising, a huge tree trunk drifted by with a man clinging to it. The man on the tree shouted for the man on the roof to jump, but the man on the roof refused, saying that God would save him. After a while, an inner tube floated by with two people on it. Again, they implored the man to join them, but he refused, saying, "God will save me." Finally, two men in a rubber boat

Chapter 11 Always Strive for More

came by and said they were there to take him to safety. The man still refused, saying, "I don't need your help because God will save me." Eventually, the man drowned, and when he got to heaven, he was very upset. He asked God, "Why did You not save me?" God looked at the man and said, "I sent you so many opportunities to be saved, why did you not take them?"

Remember this story throughout your life because most of your best opportunities will not look like you want them to. They may be wrapped up in hard work, long hours, dirty overalls, and who knows what else. You need to be willing to do what it takes to make the most of every opportunity.

Some of my greatest growth in my life came when I grabbed those difficult opportunities that lay outside my comfort zone. These were things that I had no idea how to do, but I did them anyway. And the more I did, the better I got. Don't let the fear of the unknown keep you from doing something.

"A pessimist sees the difficulty in every opportunity; an optimist sees the opportunity in every difficulty."

Winston Churchill

Chapter 11   Always Strive for More

Number five: Never ever quit.

There may come a time that it feels like everything is just too much, that it is all becoming too overwhelming, and you may feel like you want to quit. We have all been there. It's OK to feel like quitting. The key is not to allow yourself to quit.

There is a saying that night is darkest before the dawn. When things in your life seem the darkest they have ever been, then remember that your dawn is just around the corner. It is just about to break the horizon and spring forth as a new day. Tough times never last, but tough people do.

If you make the conscious choice never to quit, then you are unbeatable. You might get knocked down today, but you will get up, dust yourself off, review your mistakes, learn your lessons, and come back stronger.

You don't keep practicing until you can do it, you keep practicing until you can do it so well that you can no longer fail. You just keep getting better.

"You just can't beat the person who never gives up."

Babe Ruth

Remember that quitting is easy, that is why most people do it. If you want to be successful, it is imperative that you don't get sucked into the habit of quitting. I once heard a story about a man who found gold on a piece of land. He started mining the gold and made some money. After a while, the

Chapter 11   Always Strive for More

vein of gold just stopped. The man kept digging deeper and deeper, but he couldn't find the gold vein again. Eventually, he sold the land to someone else for a measly sum of money. The new owner promptly called in some experts and they found the main vein just a few feet away from where the first owner was digging, and it was a rich vein, indeed.

You see this story, which I believe is a true story, has a couple of lessons to teach us. Firstly, don't just blindly jump into something without getting proper advice from experts. Make sure that you have researched every aspect of a situation before making a decision about the future of that project. Secondly, don't get so caught up in your success that you think you can't learn anything new. And thirdly, don't quit.

Don't quit before you even try. That is the only true failure, never trying in the first place. And once you try something, keep trying until you get it right. Everything in life takes practice.

You need to become known as the most resilient, hardworking, and patient person your friends have ever met. Keep going, keep learning, keep growing, never quit, and you will see your success.

"Success is not final, failure is not fatal. It is the courage to continue that counts."

Winston Churchill

Chapter 11 Always Strive for More

In conclusion, you may be going through some challenges right now, and you will again in the future. What you need to do is stay strong and remain positive. Surround yourself with people that can uplift you. Be willing to teach others, and be willing to work with others to reach mutual success. Never stop learning. Constantly strive to improve yourself, and never ever quit.

I truly hope that through this book, you will find your strength and self-worth, and that you will realise that you have so much to offer this world.

Remember, to Jesus, you are worth dying for. It might have been thousands of years ago, but it is just as relevant today as it was back then. You are so much more valuable than you give yourself credit for. You are precious in the sight of God!

God bless you!

Breaking the Zone

Breaking the Zone

Breaking the Zone

Acknowledgement

I have spent a couple of years contemplating this book and what I might put into it. I can truly say that I have been remarkably blessed in my life. Through every life challenge, I learned new things, I gained new experiences, and I have been able to grow into a man that I never really thought I could be.

Throughout my life, there has always been one thing that always kept me going, that always picked me up when I hit rock bottom, and that always gave me strength when I needed it most. Jesus Christ has always been there for me whenever I needed him. I may not have always felt Him, but I know He was there. Looking back on my life right now, I can see His hand in every situation, lifting me up and helping make things turn out for good. I truly want to thank my Saviour for always being there for me.

Secondly is my wonderful wife. Her support since the day I met her has always helped me to see myself as the man I so longingly wanted to be. Her unconditional love has kept me going when things got so bad that I felt like crying. She always supported me even when the entire world seemed to be standing against me. Thank you, my angel. I love you.

I want to thank every single mentor that has helped me along my way. Some of you I have never even met, except only through audio tapes or online videos, but the value you added and the impact you had on my life will never be forgotten.

Lastly, I would like to thank every single individual that I have ever come in contact with. Whether it was a good experience or a bad experience, I want to thank you. There are too many of you to call by name, but without each and every one of you, I would not have been able to be the man I am today. You made me stronger.

Thank you all!

Love,
Pieter

Breaking the Zone

Breaking the Zone

About the Author

Pieter Van Der Westhuizen was born as the youngest of five children in a small mining village near Witbank on the Highveld of Mpumalanga, South Africa. Pieter grew up as a very shy boy and because of his shyness, he always felt like he struggled to fit in. Pieter, however, loved the outdoors and spent most of his spare time in the forest surrounding the village. He spent many years teaching himself how to overcome his shyness. This led to many achievements throughout his life. By the age of 34, Pieter had worked as a Boilermaker Artisan for more than 12 years, as a project buyer and he has spent time in the military as command post assistant and radar operator in both the South African Army and Air Force. Pieter also holds a private pilot's license and is a licensed financial advisor.

After a devastating head-on car accident in September 2009, Pieter had to radically re-shape his life. Since then, he has become the first Ziglar Legacy Certified Trainer in Africa and has been involved with motivational speaking and coaching since 2012. Pieter has an incredible insight into what makes people function at their peak and he is very passionate about making a difference in the world, while helping others to achieve more. Pieter believes that with God all things are possible and he lives his life that way.

www.BreakingTheZone.com

Breaking the Zone

Breaking the Zone

Disclaimer & Copyright Information

Some of the events, locales, and conversations have been recreated from memories. In order to maintain their anonymity, in some instances, the names of individuals and places have been changed. As such, some identifying characteristics and details may have changed.

Although the author and publisher have made every effort to ensure that the information in this book was correct at press time, the author and publisher do not assume and hereby disclaim any liability to any party for any loss, damage, or disruption caused by errors or omissions, whether such errors or omissions result from negligence, accident, or any other cause.

All quotes, unless otherwise noted,
are attributed to the respective Authors or to the Holy Bible.

Cover illustration, book design and production
Copyright © 2017 by Tribute Publishing, LLC
www.TributePublishing.com

Scripture references are copyrighted by www.BibleGateway.com which is operated by the Zondervan Corporation, L.L.C.

Breaking the Zone

www.ingramcontent.com/pod-product-compliance
Lightning Source LLC
Chambersburg PA
CBHW021128300426
44113CB00006B/338